SNATCHED

THE CHOSEN TRILOGY

CHEYENNE NIKOLE,
ELISABETH FOWLER

Book cover created by Ghost Rock Design.

ISBN: 979-8-85-621416-0

To all of The Chosen Trilogy readers,
may the Most High bless you and keep you always.

The righteous perisheth, and no man layeth
it to heart: and merciful men are taken away,
none considering that the righteous is taken
away from the evil to come.

Isaiah 57:1

ONE

SOLO

Drea had officially gone AWOL.

I mindlessly swiveled in my chair, unsure how to piece together the puzzle behind her bizarre motives. All the slip-ups and set-downs didn't even faze that woman. She was determined to cause as much mayhem as possible in everything she did.

Now, her running away from the Sanctuary represented the ultimate betrayal not only because she abandoned the people who protected her but also her own child. Little Isaiah didn't deserve that from his sporadically detached mother, nor did we.

I needed an update.

I was itching for a visual of the mission, and I desperately wanted to be part of the action...part of the team, but it was too late to shove the drone into anyone's hands before the group bounded off in search of Drea.

Without the eyes of the drone, I was limited to blindly listening to Raya's heavy breathing through her comms while she and the others sprinted through the woods.

With my face glued to the monitor, I stared at the displayed aerial view of the forest surrounding the team. To guide them to Drea's location accurately, I had no choice but to watch her analog locket beacon mockingly blink back at me. I wished all this was a terrible mistake, a dream turned rancid, but there she was, her absence a persistent reminder on the screen.

Drea weaved through the dense pockets of autumn foliage, proving how legitimately lost she was, both physically and mentally, but eventually, the black dot stopped moving across my screen.

"Veer to the east. She stopped about half a mile out," I instructed Raya through her special radio comms.

I was so glad I had completed her communicator upgrades before this chance mission, making them resistant to the elements and to her own sweat. It would've been useless to both of us if the mole comms accidentally slid off her face from all the exertion.

A nagging feeling began tugging at the back of my thoughts—something foreboding, maybe a warning.

"Raya, please be careful," I pleaded into my headset when that feeling enveloped me.

She didn't return an answer, but I could hear an abundance of body contacts, punches, kicks, and groans emitting from her comms.

I instantly imagined the worst—Syndicate soldiers must have found them while looking for Drea.

This isn't good. None of them have any weapons.

Two sharp cracks of delayed gunfire pierced through my headset, jolting me to my feet. In surprised confusion, I searched around the Lookout, anxiously checking for the source of the sound. The shots, unnervingly loud and proximate, triggered a sicking realization. I was hearing gunfire through Raya's comms, leaving me with an unsettling sense of indecision.

Should I risk it and go as backup?

"Raya—" I bellowed.

I sat back down, then popped back up nervously. I walked around in a tight circle, my hands clasped to my head, wondering what was happening above ground.

"Raya!" I called out again with no response.

I heard Naomi screaming nonstop in the background. After a few more agonizing minutes, I decided I had about enough of anxious waiting.

That's it!

I removed the headset and stormed towards the vault to get a weapon. I was going up top.

I heard a faint cry for help as I passed the laundry room, stopping me dead in my tracks.

Big Man popped his head out the doorway, holding a soaking-wet pair of jeans.

He looked at me and asked, "Did you hear that?"

"I think so," I cautiously replied.

"Shh. Listen, listen. There it is again—sounds like someone is screaming for help," Big Man whispered.

The cries kept getting louder and closer.

Big Man dropped the sopping wet jeans to the floor and took off running towards the tunnel's exit side where the call originated. I abandoned my trip to the vault and followed suit, fast on his heels.

"HELP! SOMEBODY HELP PLEASE!" we heard James frantically calling out through labored panting.

We reached him halfway down the exit leg of the tunnel.

As we got close, James stopped running and looked like he was about to keel over from exhaustion. He huffed, trying to catch his breath, then pointed towards the exit hatch.

"It's Juda..." he barely got out.

There was no hesitation. We all ran for the hatch.

Big Man got to the runged ladder first and immediately went up and out. A few seconds later, he descended with

Juda, cradling his flaccid body in his massive arms. James went behind him to secure the hatch.

When I first glanced at my cousin, he looked like a peacefully sleeping child, but Juda had a hole in his head, and his breathing was sparse and ragged.

I recalled hearing the two loud gunshots coming through Raya's comms, but Juda's head wound only accounted for one of those shots.

Raya wasn't responding over the radio, and my heart was pounding through my chest.

I silently prayed that the other bullet wasn't meant for her.

Is she dead?

I turned and began screaming for Adina while searching for her through the other side of the tunnel. I didn't have to go far because she was already in her newly constructed Infirmary on the right wing of the corridor.

She popped out into the walkway and looked towards me with alarmed confusion in her eyes.

"I'm right here, Solo. What's going on?" she questioned, startled by my panic.

I turned and pointed down the left wing of the tunnel.

"It's Juda...he's been shot," I rasped, hoarse now from the hollering.

She immediately took off, running past me towards the exit. She didn't have to go far because Big Man and James rounded the corner with Juda stretched out in Big Man's arms.

When she reached them, she took one look at Juda's perforated skull and commanded, "Take him to the Infirmary!"

While she and Big Man moved with purpose towards the med room, I didn't have the courage to follow.

Instead, I turned to James and frantically asked him what happened.

As he spoke, I felt a tightness in my chest that strangled the air from my lungs. My palms were getting sweaty, and dizziness tried to overpower my senses. Every word that entered my brain took twice as long for me to grasp. My thoughts were in overdrive.

I needed to calm down.

I tried to take slow, deep breaths as his voice rose and fell in his descriptions. I was in full, pessimistic anticipation of learning Raya's fate.

He explained the whole scene, and to my immediate relief, I learned that it wasn't Raya who received the other bullet.

But to my horror, I discovered that it was Ryan on the receiving end and that he was still out there, with more Syndicate soldiers on their way to dispose of him.

I knew I had Drea's tracking locket still showing on my monitors, and Raya's comms were still on. I could easily track them down, but Ryan would die if we didn't prioritize him first.

"I have to go get him before they do," I decided out loud.

James nodded his head in agreement and said he was coming, too.

The vault was only a few feet away, so we rushed there first for weapons.

James grabbed a rifle and a Bowie knife, and I reached for the nearest 9mm pistol. After securing the vault shut, we sprinted for the exit.

When we reached the end of the tunnel, I climbed up the ladder and swiveled the hatch door open, letting the light of day filter down on us.

I prayed to the Most High[1] we weren't too late.

---

1. God

Two

—— ✤ ——

Angel

I TOSSED MY CANVAS overnight bag onto the crackled leather bench seat of the old black Ford pickup. After scooching in behind the large steering wheel, I looked back at the ornate mailbox, realizing I would never see it again.

It was dusk, and I needed to put as much distance between me and here as possible. Looking at the ancient fold-out map, I traced my intended route in my mind's eye.

If I headed south on I-65, I could connect to I-10 and continue west all the way to Houston.

My tank was already full of gas, and I could pull over somewhere in Mississippi or Louisiana to fill up again.

If I didn't need to stop repeatedly, I would make it within ten hours.

I would be there at first light.

I prayed for traveling mercies and put the truck into drive, kicking up dust from the dirt road as I put my foot down heavily on the accelerator.

THREE

— ◆ —

SOLO

WE DIDN'T HAVE TIME to get to the ATVs, so James and I ran as fast as we could back to the scene of Juda's altercation.

James led the way and was pouring sweat from all the exertion. He looked faint but kept the pace at full speed, knowing we had little time to waste.

I silently prayed again that we weren't already too late.

The rhythmic movement of my legs towards a goal, towards a purpose, temporarily filled my thoughts and pushed aside all recollection of Juda lying there in Big Man's arms, dying.

When James slowed to an exhausted stop, he bent forward and grasped his knees, trying to catch his breath. He could only point forward, wagging his finger to go ahead.

I looked forward and saw a flash of blue walking through the trees, so I angled myself behind a massive oak.

From my limited view, I noted three soldiers approaching Ryan's unconscious body.

They had not seen or heard us running towards them for their loud conversation.

"Look what we got here!" a cropped brunette soldier hooted.

He flipped Ryan over with his boot.

Ryan's arms splayed out, and the whole front side of him was covered with dirt and debris.

"Should we tie him to a tree and do a little target practice?" laughed a red-headed soldier.

He had a significant gap between his two front teeth and was shorter than the other two. His blue camo uniform bunched around his ankles and wrists as if they were standard issued, and he was much below standard.

"Nah. Use a proper gun and just put him out of his misery right here and now," spoke a blonde-haired soldier. "We don't have time to be playing around in the woods. I'm ready to get some burgers going on the grill."

His long hair was tied back into a ponytail. He reminded me of one of Raya's old Ken dolls with the perfect features and fake smile plastered on his face.

"I thought Allen said there were two bodies out here," the brunette questioned skeptically.

He began searching through the fallen leaves to pick up any additional traces of a struggle.

"Yeah...he said he got 'em in the head, too. Either he lied, or we got a zombie on our hands," Blonde Ken sarcastically answered.

The short, red-headed one slapped his thigh and laughed hysterically before he jokingly added, "Allen is always telling tall tales over something. Last week, he told me he caught a bluefin tuna in the Chattahoochee."

"Okay?" Blonde Ken responded cynically.

"It was a rainbow trout...bluefins don't even come up this way this time of year...and besides...they're in the ocean. He's just an idiot," RedHead retorted. "He probably can't even count to two, much less shoot two...especially not square in the head."

"No...there were two. Here's some more blood spatter over here," Brunette answered, pointing to the spot where Juda must have dropped.

James was disengaging the safety on his rifle behind his own oak tree while the soldiers argued about the missing second body.

I did likewise, and we covertly stepped out into the clearing.

James had caught his breath and was ready for action. He fired a round at Redhead, striking him in the back.

One down.

I fired two low, succinct shots at Blonde Ken, striking him once in each knee. He cried out in anguish and surprise at being downed by an unexpected person coming from behind the trees.

The brunette soldier was a little quicker than I had anticipated, but his aim was off. He fired a round at me, but it whizzed by, knocking a small plot of bark from the tree to my left.

This gave James plenty of time to aim and return fire.

Brunette was struck in the neck and fell immediately to the ground, spitting blood on his way down while gripping tightly at his wound.

Blonde Ken was writhing on the ground in pain and yelling, "You shot me!" repeatedly.

I approached him and put pressure on his right knee with my black tennis shoe.

He immediately responded in screams of pure agony.

"I can help you...but you're gonna have to help me first," I bargained, with my foot still on his shattered knee.

He nodded his head rapidly in compliance.

"Tell me...is there an antidote to those stupid bullets y'all keep shooting us with?" I demanded.

He shook his head 'no'.

I pressed down on his knee with my foot, somehow suspecting he was lying.

He yelped out and said, "Okay, okay! Take some aspirin! Take some aspirin. You got to thin out the blood."

"Do you have any?" I further enquired.

He hesitated but shook his head 'no' again. He cringed, expecting me to put more pressure on his wound, but when I didn't, he relaxed his face.

James tore off two strips of fabric from the hem of his shirt and tied one tightly around each of Blonde Ken's thighs.

He yelped each time.

James then grabbed one of his arms, and I held onto the other, and we drug him through the woods, as close to the main road as we felt safe to take him.

"You can make it from here," I indifferently said as we heard cars driving nearby.

I reached down, pulled his two-way radio out from his cargo side pocket, and patted him down to ensure he didn't have any other weapons to sneak attack us with once we turned our backs to him.

Satisfied with his care, we took off at a fast pace back to where Ryan and the two other soldiers lay.

When we returned to the clearing, the soldiers were already turning blue in the face. We knew then that there was no use in trying to help them.

I grabbed Ryan and gingerly picked him up, shifting his weight across my right shoulder. He was heavier than I predicted, and I wished we had time to get an ATV.

Transporting him that way would have been much easier and quicker.

I ambled for what felt like an eternity, with him slung over my shoulder, to the Franklin tree, then bent down stiffly to put in the code without letting go of him.

James swiveled the hatch open when the whirring and groaning sounds indicated the door could be accessed.

He went down first.

I lowered Ryan's limp body to him, and he took over, carrying him the rest of the way.

We finally got him to the Infirmary and laid him across one of the med beds to be triaged next.

I glanced over at Adina, who was struggling to think of ways to help Juda.

She looked at a complete loss while wildly flitted about him, checking his vitals.

She eventually turned to me then gazed down at Ryan with her forehead puckered in thought.

"Where was he shot?" she questioned briefly.

"In the back," James replied.

She nodded and turned her attention back to Juda, knowing Ryan had more time and would likely survive the chemical attack on his nervous system.

Juda's breathing was becoming more labored.

"Do we have any aspirin here?" I asked her, hoping the soldier's intel was good.

"No, we don't, and I just took a blood sample from him. It's coagulating like sludge. He won't be able to endure this much longer. Aspirin would be beneficial to thin out his blood if we had any. What made you think of that?" she hastily questioned.

"One of the Syndicate soldiers told me that aspirin is the only thing like an antidote to their bullets," I replied.

She looked at me curiously as if trying to figure out how I had an actual conversation with a Syndicate soldier, but she didn't bother asking.

We both knew there was no time.

"If I could get some medicinal plants from the woods, I think I can reverse this...if you're saying all we need is aspirin," Adina declared, already picking up her canvas shoulder bag and a scalpel from the med supply closet.

"I'm going with you," Big Man volunteered to Adina.

With everything going on, I had completely forgotten he was in the room.

Being so hyper-focused on my cousin's condition, I didn't even notice him crouched in the corner like a ninja.

James handed him the rifle and Bowie knife as he exited the room.

"I'm going, too," I blurted out, not wanting to stay in the Infirmary just to hear Juda choking on his own breath.

I needed to do something.

Anything.

"I'll go get Elijah. He needs to know," James said as everyone else retreated towards the exit.

As soon as we made it to the hatch, I heard loud crackling on the soldier's two-way radio that was still in my back pocket.

"Bill, come in. Over," the radio screeched. "Bill...Randy...Tim? Come in. Over."

The line got quiet, and I could only imagine more soldiers converging on our woods in search of their missing comrades. I turned the radio off and threw it as far away into the trees as I could possibly manage.

"We need to head south, away from where they're gonna end up," I stated.

"What are we looking for, again?" Big Man asked, cautiously scouting our surroundings with his rifle partially aimed.

James had left the safety disengaged for him.

"I need to find a White Willow tree and some Pipsissewa plants," Adina denoted like we knew what she was talking about.

"Well, can you please explain what they look like so I can be on the lookout, too?" I asked, wanting to get whatever it was and get back to the Sanctuary immediately.

Adina thought about correctly describing the tree she needed before she settled on, "Think Weeping Willow with a two-toned leaf. The long leaves are a lighter or whiter shade on the backside."

I pulled on every remnant of memory I could muster about hiking through these woods.

"I think there is something like that near the pond," I finally recollected.

"Then lead the way. We need to hurry. Juda has, maybe, a few more hours of fight left in him," she solemnly theorized.

We wasted no time hiking the nearly four miles towards the pond. As tired as I was, my adrenaline rose to the occasion and helped me push through.

I prayed earnestly that we would not meet with any more Syndicate soldiers. I had encountered enough shootouts for the day.

Miraculously, we didn't spot any blue movement in the woods. The ones that patrolled this part must have responded to the search for the missing three in the opposite direction of us.

Big Man paused abruptly and raised his rifle.

Adina and I stopped in our tracks.

When a large raccoon popped out of some brush and scurried by, Big Man lowered his weapon, and we continued in silence.

Occasionally, Adina would bend down and pick some small growing plants off the woodland floor. I didn't understand how she could tell one plant from another.

All I could distinguish while out in the woods was either leaf or limb, green or brown.

The plants she kept picking at were barely visible, green-leafed things with a strip of white down the middle and sported pointed tips. The flowers were pinkish-white and looked like an umbrella but upside down.

"What is that?" I asked her quietly, not purposefully trying to break her concentration.

"It's Pipsissewa. Some people call it bitter wintergreen or Prince's Pine. It will help detox the poison from his liver and kidneys," she responded while maintaining eye contact with the ground.

Once satisfied with the substantial bundle she had gathered, we picked up the pace until we ran into the White Willow tree.

Adina carefully studied it, then took out her scalpel and cut away several young branches at their nodes. The tree was massive and looked fairly established, so it was unlikely to suffer much from her impromptu surgery.

When she was content with her collection of smaller branches, she asked Big Man for his Bowie knife and commenced stripping some of the older-looking bark from the main trunk after he handed it over.

She stuffed everything in her bottomless canvas satchel and told us she was ready to head back.

When Adina began walking back the way we came, I reached out and grabbed her arm to stop her.

"We're closer to the entrance hatch. It's safer to go back this way," I directed.

She nodded in compliance, and I led them in the opposite direction.

Big Man saw the second Franklin tree immediately.

He stopped and bobbed his head, laughing.

"Your uncle was a very sapient man," he commented, with a smile still on his face.

I nodded slowly.

I would have to look that word up when we got back to the Sanctuary, but I assumed it meant thoughtful or something like that from how he said it.

I pulled the single white flower lever in the middle of the tree, and the groaning and clicking of the hatch lock signaled that it was disengaged.

I reached under the tree and opened the hatch.

I looked to Adina and offered, "After you."

She blinked a 'thank you' and went down first, then Big Man descended.

I went last, satisfied that we weren't being followed.

Praise AHAYAH[1] , we made it back safely.

I said a quick prayer under my breath for Juda to continue enduring.

It was a selfish thought, but I couldn't help thinking that Juda had no right to leave me all alone.

Raya was gone, and he was all I physically had left.

We ran the whole three miles through the tunnel back to the heart of the Sanctuary.

When we stepped breathlessly back into the Infirmary, there was a medium-built woman, who appeared to be in her late thirties, sitting attentively next to Juda. Her skin was copper-brown, her hair was tightly covered in a green headwrap, and she sported matching green medical scrubs.

---

1. one Hebraic variation of the name of the Most High; God- Exodus 3:14

Juda had an IV in his left arm with a saline drip bag attached. She had rigged a metal stand to hold the line like they do at hospitals, and she was checking his pulse with a stethoscope.

When she heard our footsteps approaching, she swiveled her head towards us and removed her stethoscope from her ears.

She addressed Adina first.

"Why, hello. You must be Adina. Brother Elijah informed me that you may need some assistance. My name is Mira," she calmly explained. "I'm an LPN."

"Oh, praise the Most High!" Adina frantically exclaimed, with tears of relief dampening her eyelashes.

Mira gave us all a reassuring smile and continued, "This young man needed some aspirin according to...James. I think that's what he said his name was. I happened to have a few left in the bottom of my purse, but it's not enough, I'm afraid. I bought him some time, but he needs more. I started him on some fluids. He's gonna need it and plenty more to flush his system...James so kindly explained about the chemical bullets."

"I brought some White Willow bark from the woods and other herbs to make some tinctures and teas, but he needs a nasogastric tube so I can get it into him," Adina advised.

Mira turned to a large blue duffle bag she had placed near Juda's bed and started pulling out medical supplies.

She pulled out a plethora of different-sized tubing, more bags of saline fluid, and even a bedpan.

"I was supposed to head to a hospice patient of mine within our church body...she was due a medical care delivery after our Shabbat service...but those blue camo clowns attacked us in the parking lot on our way out."

Mira focused demurely on Big Man.

"If it had not been for y'all, I probably would have been dead. From what young James mentioned, those chemicals can kill people with serious illnesses, and I struggle with Lupus. It's what inspired me to get into nursing in the first place. Now...enough about me. Let us begin."

Adina explained that she would go make the concentrated Willow bark tea and asked if Mira could prep Juda for administration.

Mira mentioned that he would also need a catheter and additional wound care for his head, which she would see to as well.

Adina nodded in agreement and sprinted out of the room towards the kitchen.

I introduced myself to the older woman and explained my relation to Juda.

"This must be really hard on you to witness...but have faith, young man. Yah[2] Almighty can do wondrous miracles if you just step out of His way," she said with great sagacity.

I agreed and turned towards Ryan, lying in the bed adjacent to Juda.

Someone had cleaned his face and changed his shirt.

"I'll make sure he gets some Willow tea, too, when your friend comes back," Mira said, anticipating my concerns.

Raya!

Without another word, I took off towards my Lookout room, not bothering to say goodbye.

When I got in, I pulled up Drea's locket beacon and saw she was moving quickly along I-10, headed west.

I put my headset on and breathed a prayer that Raya would answer me.

"Raya? Raya...Raya!"

I heard her rhythmic breathing.

She sounded as if she was...taking a nap.

After calling her name repeatedly for what seemed like eons, I finally heard a groan and then a strained whisper.

"Solo?"

---

2. name of the Most High; God- a variation

"Yes! Raya...are you okay? What's going on?" I squeaked out.

She ignored me and started to whimper and cry for Juda, saying he was dead over and over. She became dementedly loud as she called out for her brother.

Before I could confirm that he was alive and currently being treated, I heard a loud electronic crackling in my headset, setting my ears abuzz.

In pain, I lifted the headset but quickly readjusted it and revealed that he was alive.

"Raya, did you hear me? Raya!" I called out, but she didn't reply.

She didn't speak anymore, but I could hear her labored breathing again.

I rechecked Drea's locket location and saw that they had crossed the border of Alabama into the southern tip of Mississippi.

I didn't have to wonder.

I knew exactly where they were headed.

It would take them another three hours to get to Ocean Springs...to get to the TRP.

FOUR

— ◆ —

RAYA

Raya! Raya...Raya?

The back of my head was throbbing, and my arms were extended behind me, still tied. My hands were starting to tingle from being trapped in the same position for so long.

Before I could even open my eyes good, I heard Solo invading my thoughts, calling my name.

"Solo?" I rasped, coming out of my stupor.

"Yes! Raya...are you okay? What's going on?" he said, rather emotionally.

Then, everything was crystal clear again.

The last thing I remembered was Juda's dead eyes, staring at me, accusing me.

A ripple of torment rushed through me in a wave of affliction and pulled me under like a riptide.

I was forced to feel it and own it in all its raw state of bitterness.

I couldn't focus on Solo.

I couldn't hear him or appreciate his words.

But my own voice grew in anguish as I mourned for my brother, who wanted nothing more than to keep me safe.

The same soldier that had shot and killed Juda emerged before me and struck me in the left side of my face with the butt of his rifle.

"Shut up!"

He struck me hard enough for compliance but not enough to knock me out again, and I obliged.

There was no point in even trying to fight back.

I laid my head down on the metal windowsill of the white prison bus. It was the exact same kind that we had narrowly escaped from just a few months prior.

The window was partially down, and the air was not as cool as I would have expected for October, but the fresh air was welcomed.

I looked out towards the sun, which was high in the sky and in front of us.

From what Dad had taught us about surviving in the wilderness, I calculated that it was close to 2:30 PM.

I sat there, alone on my prison bus seat, which oddly felt like I was taking a ride to school.

I didn't hear Solo anymore, and I was almost grateful.

I didn't want to hear anyone or anything right now.

In honor of my slain brother, I wanted to wallow in my grief.

After an hour of travel like that, we hit a pothole on the interstate road. My head was banged against the windowsill forcefully, so I sat up, grimacing from the second blow.

I looked across from me to the left.

Naomi was sitting there with her hands still zip-tied behind her, and her head was bowed as if she had fallen asleep, but her eyes were still open. From what I could see of her side profile, she had dried-up tear streaks on her now dusty face. Her eyebrows were tilted angrily, and her mouth was bunched up in a tight glower.

"Naomi...hey...you okay over there?" I whispered to her.

She jerked her whole body to the left and faced her window, leaving me with only a view of the back of her head.

Her locs were full of small twigs and sandy dirt.

She didn't even attempt a reply and wholly ignored any further attempts of me trying to communicate with her.

"Hey! Shut up, I said!" the soldier at the front of the bus yelled.

I looked over at Naomi once more, then gave up.

I glanced behind me and in front of me. There were eleven other girls of various ages and heights on the bus.

They had us spaced out, so we couldn't easily communicate.

Some of the girls still sniveled and softly moaned for their families while we silently bounced up and down along the poorly maintained road.

A few rows ahead of me, I could see the top of Drea's head.

The soldiers had removed everyone's headscarves, and Drea sported a few struggle braids on each side of her head. She stared out the window the entire time.

If my hands were free, I would have lunged over the seats between us and strangled her until she fully understood my pain.

If not for her foolishness, we would all be safe in the Sanctuary, and Juda would be alive.

A hot, angry tear fell from my right eye.

After several hours of traveling, we pulled off the interstate and merged down an exit ramp toward Ocean Springs.

I saw condominiums and attractions for the ocean-front and could even smell the salt in the air now, but we passed by all the pretty buildings and hotels.

While we headed to the TRP, people stood around, carrying on with their lives.

We turned off onto a narrow road that was reminiscent of riding through swamp land.

After a few miles on the graveled, bumpy road, we approached a gray compound surrounded by tall barbed wire fencing.

The oversized sign posted on the outside of the fence read 'TRANSCENDENT RECULTURING PROGRAM' and had a symbol that almost looked like a recycling sign but consisted of six lines instead of three and had no arrows. The lines were in sets of two to make up a kind of odd triangle.

We stopped in front of the gate, and a lady soldier approached the bus and spoke to the driver, asking for his paperwork.

"Twelve, huh? Not too bad. What was your quota?" she asked the driver.

He returned a devious smile and smugly replied, "Nine."

"Excellent work, soldier. I'm sure the Commander will be generous in his reward for the extras," she mentioned, then waved him through.

A loud buzz was heard overhead, and the mechanical gate rolled open, allowing the prison bus in. It buzzed again and closed soon after the bus cleared the entrance.

I looked out of the window towards the buildings. There must have been more than twenty sections to the longest building within the compound. Each looked exactly like the next, depressing and gray.

The fencing stretched for miles. Beside the dusty grounds, it was bare of all life. On the other side of the fence were some swampy wooded areas, but even that looked like crocodiles and water moccasins would be waiting to ravage anyone who attempted an escape.

We rolled to a complete stop and parked in front of a smaller gray building marked 'Intake Center'.

Juda's murderer yelled for everyone to exit the bus quickly.

All of the females aboard complied except for Naomi. She wouldn't stand up and just kept staring out the window.

"Come on, Naomi," I whispered to the back of her head.

I stood near her seat, trying to urge her not to resist.

She still wouldn't budge.

With his rifle, the soldier marched back towards us, grabbed one of my arms, and shoved me towards the front. I had no choice but to exit the bus, leaving Naomi alone and defenseless.

He went to her next and snatched her right arm, dragging her towards the narrow aisle. She was gnashing her teeth at him and trying to kick him away when she received the first blow to the stomach with the butt of his gun.

She coughed and gasped for air while her long locs slapped her in the face.

He grabbed a handful of her hair and yanked her down the aisle while she fumbled to stay on her feet. He cast her out of the bus, letting go of her hair as she fell to the dust-filled earth.

Naomi landed on her right shoulder and continued to choke and gasp for air.

The soldier jumped past the exit steps of the bus and landed in front of her, then commenced to punching her in the face a few times for good measure.

She lay there, still quiet, but bloodied drool came out of her mouth.

He reached down and pulled on her left arm to get her to her feet.

We all looked on in horror.

"We ain't gonna have none of this fighting back mess y'all tried to pull in the woods. Around here, I'M IN CHARGE, and you do as I SAY!" he hollered. "Now, MOVE!"

We were all marched in single file into the Intake building entrance that had no door.

Once we descended a long corridor, the space opened into a sizeable warehouse-looking room.

There was a single desk with a single older white woman sporting gray-streaked hair in a neatly smoothed bun on the crown of her head. She had rosy cheeks and rounded attributes. She also wore the ugly blue camo uniform, which seemed out of place.

I would have mistaken her for a school teacher or principal under any other circumstance.

She stood up from her desk, walked back and forth before us, and began her well-rehearsed speech.

"Welcome, ladies, to the Transcendent Reculturing Program. My name is Miss Agatha. You may refer to me simply as Miss. Here, at Transcendent, you will learn your true place and value in society. You will work hard and obey all the rules, or you will find that certain actions will carry very weighty consequences. I urge you all to be on your best behavior, and with dedication and a little luck, you will be able to reintegrate back into society. You must fully complete the Program and pledge loyalty to the Syndicate and to the country, of course, but that should not be beyond anyone's capabilities. This Program is tough and rigorous but not without its rewards in the end," she lectured.

Her mature and sweet-sounding voice reverberated off the walls, but her expressions showed an underlying maliciousness.

They were subtle but very much present.

"From here, our...guides will take you to your assigned barracks. You will change quickly and use the restroom, if you must, then report back to the main yard. Your guides will be with you every step of the way," she continued, sounding extra chipper at the end.

She motioned for the soldier who brought us in to cut our zip ties off finally.

As soon as Drea's were removed, she instinctively reached for her locket.

This motion caught the attention of Miss.

"What do we have here, hmmm?" she asked, like a reprimanding school teacher.

She meandered over to Drea and stood directly in front of her.

Miss took hold of the little locket between her fingers and gently rubbed it with her thumb. Then she yanked it from Drea's neck in one smooth motion.

Drea moaned out a slight 'no'.

"What was that, dearie? I didn't quite hear you," Miss asked, cupping her right ear towards Drea.

Drea knew all too well what might await her if she actually repeated herself, so she stared at the ground instead, with her head in a deep bow.

Miss Agatha threw the locket and chain at Drea's feet, but before Drea could reach down and pick it up, she stomped on it with her booted heel and twisted it underfoot.

Drea stared at the pile of broken bits when Miss lifted her foot, and a few single tears fell from both eyes on top of the dusty remains of the locket.

Just then, six other female soldiers ascended into the room, each pulling one or two of us toward themselves.

I guessed these soldiers were to be our 'guides'.

My guide was an auburn-haired woman only a few inches taller than me. She looked to be in her late thirties, and her eyes were kind. Studying her face, I wondered how in the world she ended up being a Syndicate member.

She pointed her chin to the exit, signaling for me to walk.

I stepped past the mess the locket now was and hoped Solo saw our last location before his tracking device was smashed to smithereens.

I was the last to leave the room and did not see in which direction Naomi or Drea were taken.

The auburn-haired soldier pushed me towards a building further down the rows of barracks until we reached one marked 'M'.

She nodded her chin again to go inside.

I entered, and dozens of prison cells were on each side of the block. There was an upstairs portion that was also lined with dark-looking dungeons.

The soldier grabbed my arm and led me to a cell on the right side of the block marked 237.

So this is my new home.

M237.

Once we reached the opening, she forcefully nudged me in and closed the barred door behind me. A folded gray jumpsuit, undergarments, and a pair of gray shoes were on the top bunk bed, awaiting me.

A toilet was too close to the bed for comfort and was not partitioned with any kind of door or closure. There was also a small metal sink right next to the toilet.

I had to pee.

The soldier stared at me, then knowingly turned around, affording me a little privacy to use the toilet and change my clothes.

Once I stopped shifting around and managed to get into the provided clothes, the soldier turned back around and reopened the door.

She grabbed my old clothes from my clenched hands and walked me back toward the door. When we were almost out of the building, she aggressively threw my clothes into the large garbage barrel situated by the exit.

After we left the building, she pushed me forward into the large courtyard ahead of us.

I tripped over my too-large shoes and nearly face-planted in the dirt.

I caught myself just in time, though, and remained on my feet.

If this had happened yesterday, I probably would have given her a roundhouse kick to the face for that, but today, I didn't have anything left in me to fight for, so I kept walking toward the line of others who were already waiting in the yard.

As I joined the ranks of the other eleven ladies, I caught a glimpse of Naomi.

She was staring straight ahead; her lip was starting to swell on the left side, and she sported a deeply purple bruise under her left eye.

I wondered in which building she was housed and if I would get to see her often.

Miss joined us in the dust-filled yard and, while pacing back and forth again, explained the rules.

"Much better, ladies! These outfits will be washed once a week, and you will be issued a new uniform every Sunday. If they are damaged in any way by the end of the week, you will earn a demerit. Three demerits will cost you a day in the Chute. Four demerits, two days in the Chute...and so on and so forth. Demerits build on themselves and are never dismissed, so your reprimands will only increase from here. If you are disobedient, you will earn a demerit. If you are slothful in your work...demerit. If you are caught trying to pray to your silly little god...DEMERIT! Do you all understand? It's simple, really. Do anything untoward, and you will earn a proper punishment. Now...if you get the brilliant idea to try and escape...well, that's an automatic execution. We cannot have disorder and chaos during your stay. That just won't do, will it? Are we clear?" she harped.

We all resounded a poorly uniformed, "Yes, Miss."

No one dared to ask her what the Chute was.

"Good. Now…your first day's assignment is to stand here until it's time to get your permanent work orders at 8 AM. Welcome to the TRP. I hope you enjoy your stay," she announced with a positively obnoxious cheerfulness.

After she walked back towards the Intake building, our guides pulled out chairs a reasonable distance behind us and sat down. They began musing and taking bets on who they thought would drop first.

We could all hear them taunting us for hours after sunset. The floodlights, situated on the fencing, automatically turned on and radiated down on us in a very unnatural way.

In total, we were on our feet for thirteen hours.

Two of the females fainted after the ninth hour, and the soldiers could be heard behind us saying their 'ohhhs' and asking for their bet winnings.

I stood there, unwavering in self-punishment the entire time.

All of my thoughts were focused around Juda's accusing eyes, Mama's screams, and Dad's limp body lying in the grass.

FIVE

ANGEL

M Y TANK WAS GETTING low, and I needed to stop somewhere and refuel soon.

I hated driving through Mississippi at night, but it couldn't be avoided. I was determined to make it close to New Orleans before I stopped at a gas station.

As the 'E' popped up on the dash, I checked my location and only had three more miles to New Orleans.

I sighed a breath of relief.

I could stop now.

After another two miles, I pulled over to one of those twenty-four-hour rest stops and went inside to use the bathroom and pay cash for the gas.

As soon as I hit the doorway, the guy running the place, a young man maybe in his twenties, asked to see my ID.

I smiled, waved my passport in the air, and continued to the bathroom, trying to seem unbothered by his simple request.

I moved like I belonged there, and it was nothing for me to be inside the rest stop.

He didn't put up any further argument, so I figured I was good to go.

After using the facilities, I went to wash my hands and glanced up into the long mirror.

I could hardly recognize myself.

I had lost an incredible amount of weight and looked as skinny as a runway model. My face deepened a bit around my eyes and cheekbones, and my hair was pulled back into a messy French braid, which was not a typical style for me.

All the constant traveling in the past two and a half months had taken a toll on my body.

It would be October soon, and I needed to settle in Texas before winter began.

When I exited the restroom and approached the attendant at the counter, I saw him hanging up his cell phone.

Unbothered.

"I need $45 on 3," I requested.

He nodded and took my money with little ceremony.

I looked at him only briefly, but I noticed his cheeks turning bright red like he was embarrassed.

"Thank you, kindly," I said after he had placed my funds in the register and handed me a receipt.

He smiled slightly but didn't make eye contact with me.

I hoped this interaction wasn't what I thought it was and walked back out to the truck.

I filled up my tank, stretched my legs again, then climbed back in, determined not to make any more stops until Houston.

I took the nearby entrance ramp to I-10, westbound, and picked up a consistent speed until I was going at a stable pace, just below the limit. I drove a few un-interrupted miles until I saw the familiar red and blue flashing lights hugging my bumper.

My heart dropped into my lap, knowing the gas station clerk had phoned in my existence.

I pulled off the main road onto the shoulder and stopped cautiously. I rolled down my window and placed my hands onto the opening so the officer could see them both.

I waited a few minutes.

He was running my plates from his cruiser and corresponding with his dispatch.

When the officer finally approached, he grunted and spat at the ground before sticking his crimson face close to my window opening.

"Passport, license, and registration," he huffed.

He was three times too large for his tight uniform, and his face was ruddy from having to actually walk over to my vehicle.

I acknowledged him and stated that I was reaching into my purse to get my documents.

After handing him what he required, he returned to his patrol car to double-check everything again.

I looked in my rearview and saw him call in my document details over his two-way radio.

I sat and waited for what felt like an eternity.

I looked down at the compact .22 caliber handgun nestled into the door storage pocket. The gun and the door were both a solid black, making the firearm seem camouflaged into it.

However this encounter played out, I knew I wasn't getting out of this truck for anything or anyone.

I wasn't so concerned about my welfare, but it would be highly inconvenient to leave a messy scene on the side of the road, ditch my truck, and locate another ride.

He came back to my window and blandly handed me my documents back.

"Thank you, Ms. Merci, for your cooperation. You know...some of your people aren't as compliant," he threw in.

I smiled smugly at him and replied, "I can only imagine what you have to deal with on a day-to-day basis."

He wheezed out a laugh and told me to be safe out here at night, all alone.

I thanked him for his concern and explained that I had family nearby.

I waited until he went back to his patrol car, cut his lights off, and pulled back onto the interstate before I put my truck back into drive.

I exhaled in relief and pulled the hood of my jacket over my head, saying a prayer of gratitude to the Father in heaven above.

My passport and documents were some of the best forgeries I had seen thus far, and I was grateful to have them.

Antoine had made this last set, and although he was a computer engineer, he was multi-talented in digital art and graphic design.

I hadn't asked him about his process because I didn't want to be culpable in breaking the law.

Well...not that law.

I rode in silence the rest of the five hours to Houston, reciting scriptures to myself in my head.

Isaiah 6:8...'Also I heard the voice of the Lord, saying, Whom shall I send, and who will go for us? Then said I, Here am I; send me.'

Six

Solo

S EVERAL HOURS PASSED BEFORE I turned on the transcription feature of Raya's communications feed and rechecked Drea's location.

They reached Ocean Springs, and I was pretty sure they had made it to the TRP by now.

I saved their last known coordinates onto my hard drive.

Raya had barely spoken any words in the past three hours. I couldn't just sit here and listen to her breathing.

I transferred the data to my phablet and watched for the transcript to begin.

I needed to check on Juda and Ryan in the meantime.

I put the phablet in my pocket and walked back down to the Infirmary.

To my surprise, Ryan was sitting up in bed, sipping a dark, hot liquid from a glass mug.

"This tea is not that bad, actually," he was saying to Adina, who was sitting in a chair between him and Juda's bed. "But do you have anything for the throbbing pain in my back?"

She smiled and mentioned that there was ginger, turmeric, nettle, and cinnamon in his tea that would help with his pain.

"You need to get some rest now," she cooed.

Mira was on the other side of Juda, rechecking his vitals. She looked delighted with his progress.

"Hey," I finally said while still standing in the doorway.

Everyone looked in my direction.

"Well, hello, son. You ran out of here like you had somewhere important to be...I hope everything is okay?" Mira said, somewhat questioning me at the same time.

"His sister...my cousin... the Syndicate took her after they shot him, and I remembered that she was wearing comms. I was trying to reach her and find out what was happening with her and the others that were taken. We lost communication somehow. Her receiver is broken, but I can still hear her. According to a tracking device I planted, they've reached the TRP in Mississippi," I blurted out, wanting somebody, anybody else, to know.

Adina looked saddened but went back to adjusting Juda's IV bag.

"I'm sorry, man," Ryan said, breaking the silence. "But it's Raya...she can get out of anything. I wouldn't be surprised if she liberates the entire camp, and they come marching back in a few days."

"I don't know. When I reached out, she could hear me for a few seconds, and the way she sounded...she's different. It's like she finally snapped," I reasoned. "We need to come up with a plan to get them back."

I started thinking about everything I would need to bust someone out of a prison camp.

I would need blueprints, maps, an inside source, transportation, etc.

My brain went into overdrive, but Ryan broke me out of my concentration.

"Whatever we do, we have to do it with Juda. Let's plan, but we can't leave here without him," he decided.

I kept quiet.

I didn't think that was a smart play, but I wouldn't rain on Ryan's parade just yet.

I would keep gleaning information from Raya and see if there was a viable option for getting them out sooner rather than later.

I had never met or heard of anyone who had successfully escaped the TRP.

"Elijah called for a corporate prayer about five minutes ago if you want to join," Adina mentioned. "He didn't want to disturb you."

I nodded and walked back towards the stairs down to the community room.

A lot of people were gathered in such a short amount of time. I slipped into the back of the crowd and prepared myself to pray for Juda's recovery and Raya and the other's safe return.

SEVEN

RAYA

8 AM. MONDAY.

I blinked back the excruciating denial of sleep and waited in line to receive my work assignment.

Miss had her desk moved out to the yard.

She quickly examined us, then handed down our job assignments meticulously. As we approached, it seemed like she was searching for flaws or weaknesses within each of us.

Something she could exploit later.

When it was my turn, I was given laundry detail.

I kept my head down, not wanting her to see any emotion or care in my face. Miss moved on from me quickly, probably writing me off as a non-threat.

My auburn-haired guide led me to the laundry room to begin my eight-hour shift.

We walked through the M block of prison cells. There were some metal tables with attached stools bolted to the floor in the middle of the ample space. It seemed that where I would sleep was also where I would eventually eat.

To keep myself awake, I whispered everything I saw to myself, focusing on any and everything besides the sleep deprivation.

"Twenty cells below, twenty above, tables and stools in the middle of the corridor, bolted to the floor. No food. No water. No bathroom..." I whispered like a crazy person.

I hadn't heard Solo since the bus, so I reached up to my left temple to feel for the radio mole. When I touched it, large flecks of black appeared on the tip of my finger.

Great.

Not only was the bus soldier my brother's murderer, but he had also killed my only way to communicate with the outside world.

Guide continued to lead me through the inner door of M block and down a gray hallway that went on for about two minutes. We took a right into a room marked 'Laundry Center'.

As soon as she opened the door and ushered me in, I was hit in the face with humid heat. I could only imagine my extremely short, natural hair was coiling up on itself. No amount of gel would be able to compete with this type of thick humidity.

The air in the medium-sized room felt not only wet but sticky and was filled with a chemical-scented soap smell that reminded me of cardboard boxes after they were broken down.

Like an old pizza box.

There were five industrial-sized washing machines on the left of the room and five corresponding dryers on the right side. All of them were whirring at the same time.

On the back inner wall were two long folding tables found at laundromats. Four females, ranging in age, were moving between the machines and taking turns folding gray uniforms and undergarments. One table was filled with folded female clothes and the other with male clothes.

I didn't recognize any of the ladies in the room.

Guide pushed me in and pointed to the wall above the washing machines before leaving and slamming the door behind her.

I looked in the direction she pointed and noticed a gray poster with black words printed on it. The sign almost blended into the wall.

I read the words aloud to myself, "Laundry Room Rules. One...stay productive; slothfulness equals one demerit. Two...report all damage to authorities. If not reported, every laundry worker on duty will receive one demerit each. Three...no talking. Distracting others from their duties equals one demerit."

I watched the women mechanically move about the room for a few seconds, not knowing where to go or where to begin.

"Psst...." one of the younger girls whispered in my direction.

She then waved me over with a slight head gesture.

I took the hint and went to my left, where she was stuffing a pile of clothes into one of the middle machines. As she stooped down to push the clothes in, she did it slowly, and I clearly heard her talking to me but did not see her mouth move.

"We have to talk like this. They can't hear us on the cameras, but they can see our mouths moving."

I looked up suddenly to the corners of the room. There was a camera housed in each.

"Don't look at them! That pisses them off," she said, reaching for more dirty clothes.

I focused my eyes back on her, but I never saw her mouth move. She only spoke when in the middle of bending over or looking down.

"My name is Danielle. Folks call me Dani. I would suggest you start grabbing clothes and loading the empty machines. When the washer buzzes, one of the other ladies will take them out and load the dryers. We take turns folding. The clothes be really hot and will burn the skin right off your hands and arms if you stay over there too long. It's almost my turn. You can take my place here."

She, without warning, walked away towards the folding tables and replaced an older woman who had been folding men's clothes. The replaced lady moved over to the dryers.

They were working in a circle, starting at the washers, moving to the folding tables between the washers and dryers, and then ending up at the dryers.

I began imitating what Dani had done and bent down to pick up piles of dirty uniforms and undergarments, stuffing them inside an empty machine. There was a soap dispenser attached directly to the machine's soap intake. I figured out how the machine worked pretty quickly.

It buzzed when the cycle was done, beeped when it needed more soap and whirred and groaned from general overuse.

The dirty clothes were in piles high to the ceiling to the left of the machines and looked as if it would take a full week to wash the entire mountain, that is, if all five devices were operating twenty-four-seven.

It made me wonder just how many people were at the TRP.

Some of the clothes were darker shades of gray like the person had been playing in a coal mine. Some smelled musty, some like urine, and others like feces.

It was sickening.

After about twenty minutes of this, another lady walked up to me and nodded me to the folding table, where there was now an empty space next to Dani.

I made my way to the folding table and started folding female clothes.

"Not like that...like this," Dani breathed towards me.

She was folding the arms and legs in towards the middle of the uniform, folding them neatly onto each other until the one-piece outfit was a perfect square. She then folded the square in half and turned it over to reveal the front with the block letter and cell number on display.

I watched her do this swiftly several times before attempting it. My first one looked off-centered, but after a few tries, I mastered the fold.

As I folded, I breathed out some of the letters and numbers to myself. I started to notice that the female uniforms stopped at the letter M.

I glanced at Dani's folded piles; her letters were all N-Z.

I concluded that there were twenty-six blocks, thirteen for males and thirteen for females.

I started to understand what Dani meant by the clothes being too hot and scorching skin.

After fifteen minutes of folding, I developed a heat blister on the palm of my right hand.

"You get used to it, don't worry. After the first few blisters, your skin will get harder, and that helps repeal the pain somewhat," she uttered.

It was unnerving, yet impressive, how she talked without me ever seeing her lips move.

I was getting ready to do the fold Dani had shown me on a uniform when I noticed a worn hole in the knee.

I stared at it, not knowing what to do.

The sign said to report any damage or else we would all get a demerit, but all I could mentally picture was an elderly woman bent down on her knees all day, scrubbing a floor or a crease in the wall, causing the hole.

How could I possibly do anything to make that woman's life worse by turning her over for a demerit?

Dani must have seen the delay and dilemma whirling around in my face and head.

She yanked the uniform from me and walked over to the door, banging on it twice.

The door quickly opened, and she handed the uniform to the female soldier standing just outside the door. Dani then swiftly returned to her folding station before the door even closed to the Laundry Center.

I watched the whole interaction in unrequited horror, knowing that I, indirectly, was the cause of another person's suffering.

Dani and the other women didn't bat an eye.

They continued in their duties, and soon Dani walked away to the dryers. She stepped back and forth from the dryers to the washers, collecting wet clothes to stuff inside the dryers.

When they buzzed in completion, she lifted the overheated clothes and brought them to the folding table, where one girl began sorting them next to me.

We incessantly rotated like that for eight everlasting hours.

EIGHT

— · —

G UIDE FINALLY OPENED THE door and nodded her chin at us to move out.

She walked us down the long corridor and back through M block.

People were already seated at the tables with trays full of slop and a piece of toast, complete with a large water bottle.

Guide motioned her police baton towards the mess hall line to our right.

Everyone complied and got into the short line.

I stood behind Dani, and when it was my turn, I took a tray from the large lady behind the counter and kept moving, looking for a place to sit down.

Dani looked back at me and pointed to two empty seats across from each other.

We quickly claimed our places, and I began examining what they called food.

Half of it was indistinguishable and covered in some kind of tan gravy.

"If I were you, I would stick to the rice and bread. You can work your way up to the rest of the stuff, but if you eat it right away, it will give you some serious diarrhea...then I would have to turn you in for a demerit for soiling your precious uniform," Dani explained emotionlessly.

I nodded my head.

I had no intention of eating anything other than the bread, but since she said the mushy-looking rice was safe, I began picking at it, too.

I downed my water, not realizing how thirsty I truly was.

"Whoa, whoa, whoa," she exclaimed. "Take it slow. It's the only bottle you get for the day. You gotta save some for the morning. You can take the bottle into the cell with you, but nothing else. And if you are thinking you can just fill it up with sink water...think again. That water will give you the runs. I'm pretty sure it's swamp water...full of parasites."

I looked down at my empty bottle with instant regret.

I would know better for tomorrow, but I could do nothing about today.

"Here..." she called out and gestured towards my empty bottle.

I handed it to her, and she poured a few swallows full of her own water into mine and then handed it back.

I looked at her dumbfounded.

"Why are you helping me? I saw how you didn't even hesitate to turn in that damaged uniform," I pondered out loud.

She said between bites, "You can't help everybody, but those you can help...you should. I wish someone would have looked out for me when I first got here. I had to learn everything the hard way. I got my first demerit on my very first shift in the Laundry Center. I asked somebody what I was supposed to do and they saw me talking on the cameras. I got three demerits already, and I've only been here six weeks."

"Three demerits...already? So, you've been to the Chute?" I asked, curiosity getting the better of me.

Her whole countenance fell.

I could see wild fear behind her eyes, and she put her spork down, obviously losing her appetite.

She locked eyes with the table and replied without looking up, "Yeah...I have. And I'll do anything to avoid ever going back."

"What is it?" I pushed further.

She finally looked up and seemed to stare deep into my soul.

"It's your worst nightmare having a nightmare. They take you up on an elevator. I don't know how many floors there are, but you are on the elevator a really long time, and then when you finally get off, they lock you in this kinda box-looking thing with a seat in the middle. It's like one of those dunking booths at the county fair. They make you sit in it, and your feet are dangling in the air. There's no floor. Then they torture you nonstop."

She had a single tear fall from her left eye.

She angrily swiped at it with the back of her hand and, after a few seconds, began eating her slop again.

I stared at her but didn't ask anything else.

She finally decided to ask her own questions, "Where are you from?"

I sighed loudly and replied, "South Georgia."

She nodded.

"I'm from Louisiana. You came with any family?" she continued.

I shook my head before explaining, "I was with a group of believers in a safe place after our group was attacked during Shabbat[1] service. They shot my dad and dragged my mom away. They shot me, too, but my brother was able to get me to safety."

---

1. Saturday worship

"So, how did you end up here if you were in a safe place?" Dani asked skeptically.

She was almost finished with her meal.

"We had an incident out in the woods yesterday, and some Syndicate soldiers captured me and killed my brother..." my voice trailed off. I was losing my self-control and couldn't stop the tears from quickly filling my eyes.

"I'm sorry for your loss. What was your brother's name?" she quietly asked, still with very little emotion.

"Juda. His name was Juda," I answered, remembering Ms. Lynn's words a few months ago.

She had talked about keeping our loved ones' memories alive by talking about them often.

I would have to practice that concept for my entire immediate family.

"I have a brother named Judah, too. He's seven. I hope one day you will get to meet him," Dani replied. "And I got an older sister named Shawna. I haven't seen them since we got here, but Shawna was on the bus with me on the way here. I'm fifteen, by the way."

"What about your parents?" I asked, trying to focus on her instead of my grief.

She shook her head and answered, "We were on our way to church when we got pulled over by the cops. They asked for our passports, and when they saw my mom, sister, and I had on headscarves, they pulled us out the car, shot my parents; then next thing I knew, I was on a white bus headed here with my sister. I caught a glimpse of my dad on another bus, but it went in another direction and only had men in it."

A sick realization struck me, and I asked before I could stop myself, "Did your mom have any type of illness?"

She looked at me strangely and replied, "Yeah. She has sickle cell anemia, but hers isn't as bad as some people's. Why?"

I shook my head.

"No reason. Just asking. Maybe she was taken to a hospital instead," I quickly came up with the lie.

I didn't have the heart to explain that her mother was dead.

Then I thought about my mother.

She was healthy and would have survived the chemical bullets, but as far as I could remember, she was not injured in our first encounter with the Syndicate.

"Have you met anyone named Nora?" I asked her, craving the information. I wanted her not to be here, but I also wanted her to be here so I could see her again.

It was a strange emotional rollercoaster I was on.

Dani shook her head, "Sorry, no. But this place is huge...you can literally see a random person and then never see them again. They usually keep us close to our barracks, and we rarely ever see the opposite sex."

She got up without explanation and walked over to the mess line, giving her tray back to the woman who had handed it to her.

I got up and did the same.

"Come on...we get one free hour outside in the yard. Just don't get too close to the fence, or you'll earn yourself a demerit. Trust me...I would know."

I followed her outside and looked around.

Other people from their respective blocks were outside, but soldiers were blocking each section so no one from another block could mingle with the one next to it.

Most females at M block walked in a pathetic circle in their meager square. I joined, hoping to catch a glimpse of anything noteworthy. As I walked, I talked to myself, still reciting what I saw, but now just to pass the time.

"Miles of fencing, floodlights on every post, barbed wire, lookout towers with soldiers every twenty feet. Swampland and trees beyond the fence. Too many people to count."

After our hour was up and the soldiers announced it was time to go back inside, I lost sight of Dani. I walked to my cell, to my home...M237.

To my astonishment, a little girl was sitting on the bottom bunk, crying and rocking herself in the fetal position.

My heart sank at the sight of her.

She couldn't have been more than three or four years old.

I looked down each side of the corridor before stepping into my cell, which housed the child.

The little girl saw my taller shadow approaching and looked up.

She was startled at the sight of me, a newcomer.

Visibly terrified, she trembled in fear.

Strands of her silky waved, black hair stuck to her tear-stained cheeks.

I held up my hands as I slowly walked closer.

"It's okay... I'm not going to hurt you," I tried to reassure her. "What's the matter?"

She scooted away, attempting to press herself between the bed and the wall.

That's when I noticed the wet stain on the crotch of her uniform.

She cried out, "I don't wanna de-mor-at."

My stomach twisted in a visceral knot at her panic-stricken words. I could discern the innocence stripped away from her tiny voice, and it was shattering my heart over and over again.

Her cries began to ascend in volume by the second.

Worried that a guard would overhear and punish us both, I put my finger to my lips to indicate silence, "Shhh, it's okay...I won't tell. I promise."

She quieted but kept sucking in large gulps of air in futile attempts to calm herself.

"Let's get this off you so I can wash it in the sink, okay?" I softly directed, giving her a friendly smile to let her know I could be trusted.

She nodded sweetly and allowed me to help her remove the soiled uniform and underwear before wrapping herself up in the thin, tattered blanket that occupied her bed.

"What's your name, little sis?" I asked quietly, moving toward the sink with the clothes.

"Rio... I'm this many," she squeaked out.

I turned to see what she wanted to display.

Her pale little arm stuck out through the blanket, with four tiny fingers posing in the air.

"Rio," I repeated, "I love your name. My name is Raya. Do you mind if I stay with you from now on?"

The number on her uniform suggested that neither of us would have a choice in the matter, but I asked her all the same.

She shook her head, approving the arrangement, and smiled up at me with her perfectly aligned baby teeth.

"Well, let's get you cleaned up," I stated, then returned to scrubbing and squeezing the urine out of her too-large clothes.

NINE

—— ◆ ——

ANGEL

I PULLED OFF THE exit ramp to connect to the Sam Houston Parkway/Beltway.

The sun had already risen, and I was absolutely exhausted.

I continued for a few miles, exited, and maneuvered through a few side streets before pulling in front of a mid-sized brown duplex.

The trees were sparse in the area and were still very much green for it to be the end of September.

I parked in one of the few spaces and intently watched apartment A.

I didn't see any activity through the shaded window.

So I waited.

I put my head down on the steering wheel for just a second to rest, and when I woke up, the sun was well to the west.

I checked my watch, and it read 5:35 PM.

I looked at the apartment again and saw a light on in the window, and a shadow moved past.

I got out of my truck but left the overnight bag.

I had no idea how this exchange would go and didn't want to make assumptions about being accepted here.

I went to the duplex marked A and knocked lightly on the door.

I heard movement.

Then, a man appeared at the door a few seconds later. He was in his early thirties and had a low fade with a few gray strands popping through. His face was kind, but he looked concerned that an unexpected guest had shown up.

We weren't in the safest times for random knocks at the door, especially within our faith.

He was a few inches taller than me and looked down at me suspiciously before speaking, "Can I help you, sister?"

"Um, I sure hope so," I replied with my friendliest of smiles. "You're Jeremiah, correct?"

He nodded slowly and squinted his eyes, still trying to figure out my purpose for being at his door.

"You're Sandra's nephew, right? And your wife's name is Ava? I hope I got the right house," I continued, then coughed slightly.

"Are you okay? Do you need help? I can get Ava," he suggested.

"No, no...I'm fine. Just a little night air got me on my way in. I came because I need YOUR help. May I please come in?" I requested.

He hesitated but eventually moved back from the door and allowed me in.

After I was safely inside, he looked out the door both ways, then locked it behind him.

He led me into his comfortably sized living room and motioned that I should have a seat on the couch.

"Who was it, Jay—" his wife was saying as she came into the living room from the kitchen.

She saw me sitting on her sofa, and her words trailed off.

"Hello," she stated in my direction, then looked at her husband before continuing, "Who is this, Jeremiah?"

The way she said it was a bit accusatory, but she patiently waited for his reply before jumping to any conclusions.

"This is a friend of my Aunt Sandra. Her name is—"

"Angel. My name is Angel, and I came here for help. I've been traveling all over the United States...preparing people. I'm here, hoping to do the same in Houston. I don't know anyone personally in Texas, but I remembered Sandra speaking so fondly of the two of you. I hope you don't mind that I dropped by like this, but it's imperative," I began.

They both looked at each other, and Ava spoke up first, "Is this about all the missing people?"

I nodded.

"So you know what's happening to them?" Jeremiah followed up.

I nodded again.

"What I'm about to tell you is top secret, and in order to help stop what's happening, you will need to do exactly as I say."

I went on to explain to them about the Syndicate, their purpose, and plans.

I told them about the safe haven deep in the Sam Houston National Forest.

I gave them the coordinates of where to meet me in exactly one week's time.

I convinced them to find five people they trusted fully, tell them precisely what I just told them, then have each of those five find five people they trusted and repeat this process.

"Thank you for taking me seriously. I trust that your aunt would be very proud of you right now," I told Jeremiah, between a cough.

"Where is she, by the way?" he questioned.

"I'm not sure. She could be at any of the four TRP facilities by now. I pray for her endurance daily," I stated. "I pray for all our people's endurance and unity."

He looked solemn and glanced over to his wife as I got up to leave.

"Will you stay with us? I think it will be helpful if our people hear directly from you about all of this," Ava blurted out as I reached for the door.

I turned and faced them.

"That is very kind of you. I wouldn't mind staying with like-minded people...if it's not inconvenient, that is," I responded.

"Of course not. I just made some stew, too, if you'd like to join us," Ava urged.

I smiled at her and thanked them again for their hospitality.

I could finally break my fast.

TEN

❈

RAYA

7:30 AM. TUESDAY.

I woke up to the banging of batons on the bars of our cells and bright lights being turned on.

"Let's go, let's go, let's go. Time for work, roaches," one of the female guards yelled out at us as she passed.

She had a long, smooth, black ponytail pulled tightly to the back of her head. Her skin was rather tan to be inside with us all day, and she wore dark shades...inside.

I wondered what work detail she oversaw.

Whatever it was must have been outside.

I jumped down from my top bunk to check on Rio and use the bathroom.

I had cleaned her uniform and underwear the best I could, and it seemed they dried quite well while hanging from the bars between our beds overnight.

I had used all of my remaining strength to wring out as much water as possible, and it appeared to have done the job.

After relieving my own bladder, I helped Rio use the toilet and then dressed her in the now-dry clothes. We rolled the sleeves and pants up considerably since it was an adult standard-issue uniform.

She smiled slightly at me but didn't say much.

I could only imagine what horrible things this child must have seen and endured to soil herself like that.

She seemed very bright and intuitive for a four-year-old. Under normal circumstances, I wouldn't think she would have had a bedwetting issue.

"No bad dweems," she stated to herself as she waited by the locked, barred door.

I looked out and across into the other cells, and everyone else was standing in the same manner as Rio. They were stationed near the bars and facing the corridor in between the rows of cells.

Rio turned around and reached for my hand.

She pulled me next to her, then swiftly let go of my hand. She went back to staring outside of the barred door.

A loud buzzing sound occurred, and simultaneously, all the doors opened.

Rio turned to me again, but this time, she waved good-bye and moved towards the front door, towards the yard. It did not take long for her to disappear down the dusty path towards the Intake Center, out of my sight.

I shuffled towards the back of the building, seeing people lining up to complete their respective work assignments.

When I saw Dani, I fell into place behind her.

I tried to whisper a greeting to her, but she ignored me and stayed utterly silent, with her head lowered.

We were led down the hallway and, to the right, back to the Laundry Center. Guide banged on the door, and it swung open within mere seconds.

A line of five other women meandered out, and Guide ushered us, the new five, in.

Guide left with the spent women in tow.

Instead of turning left towards M block, she led them straight down the hallway. As they passed, I saw that all their uniforms were marked by the letter H.

I didn't recognize any of them, but one girl caught my eye. She was light-skinned, likely in her early twenties, and her hair was cornrowed into a bun, secured at the crown of her head. Her eyes were piercing, and she looked...angry. She quickly turned her gaze back to the ground and continued down the hallway.

I wondered where all these people hailed from.

Dani wasn't kidding when she said this place was huge.

As soon as we entered the hot, moist room, everyone began working immediately, taking over where the prior five left off.

My limbs were sore from yesterday's haul, but I had no choice but to keep up.

Dani continued to be quiet, not risking any slip-ups today. She put extra effort into her tasks and kept her head down the entire day.

I was forced to do the same, with no distraction of conversation. None of the other women spoke to me or each other. This confused me because I heard everyone doing their ventriloquistic acts just yesterday.

By the end of our shift, a total of four uniforms were reported.

Various women, including Dani, went up to the door each time, banged twice, and then handed over the evidence of infraction when the door opened to them. Then, they quickly went back to work.

By the time the guard banged on the door, signaling that our time was up, my entire left hand was bubbled in razor-sharp heat, and my right hand was not far behind.

What I wouldn't give for some creamy lavender balm.

We lined up speedily and were led out by a husky blonde-haired woman with a buzzcut.

From her demeanor, I had no issue discerning that she was not a fair or kind person.

She inspected us thoroughly while we walked and had a devilish look about her face like she took joy in lording over others.

Everyone stared at their shoes as we were taken back down to our block.

Once we got to M block, it was the same routine of grabbing a tray of food and then locating a seat.

I wondered if I had offended Dani in some way yesterday, but as soon as I sat down, she followed suit right across from me.

"Tuesdays are the worst," she began.

I looked at her while she dug her spork into the tan gravy and rice. I picked at the corners of my slice of white bread and began popping them into my mouth, trying to savor the act of eating.

I was used to fasting, and true hunger pains had not reached me yet, but with a few more days like this...it would be inevitable.

I wondered to myself how many more days I had left in me until I could no longer avoid eating the slop.

"Karen watches the cameras on Tuesdays. She swears she can see us talking, and if you take even a second to rest, she will give you a demerit. She will give you a demerit for looking at her wrong or not answering fast enough. That lady is on a serious power trip," she further explained.

"You mean the guard that just brought us in?" I asked.

She nodded, "Yeah, you gotta be careful on Tuesdays."

She went back to shoveling slop into her mouth.

I looked at her and couldn't help but study her features. She came off much more mature for a fifteen-year-old, but her face showed her actual age.

I was sure the humidity in the laundry room helped her skin stay supple, at least.

Her hair was in eight neat cornrows and tied together demurely at the nape of her neck. Her skin was a warm shade of burnt copper, and her eyes were almost onyx. She was roughly my height, and her build was on the smaller side, probably due to the lack of proper nutrition.

Her facial features were nothing striking, but she had bushy eyebrows, which gave her a modelesque appearance.

"Tell me more about your safe place," she somewhat demanded.

"There's not much to tell, and it would bore you anyways, but I wanna hear more about you though," I answered. "What about your Judah and your sister, Shaw-na?"

I liked Dani, but I wasn't sure if I could trust her because of her zeal to turn people in for demerits.

And if she got another demerit, she'd be tortured again and would most likely try to bargain information in exchange for it to stop.

I couldn't risk it.

"Judah is so annoying," she laughed slightly, looking off in the distance. "But what I wouldn't give to hear him calling for me to play with him one more time."

I nodded knowingly.

I reminisced over all the arguments me and my brother had, all the sparring sessions he had lost against me, and all the times he tried to protect me.

"My sister is nineteen. Since my mom has sickle cell, it was really rough on her to have kids, you know? We had such huge gaps between us that we didn't really get along that well because of the age difference. Now, there are so many things I regret not telling my brother and sister. I hope they know I love them," she said despondently.

I felt terrible for making her trudge up so many hurtful memories and regrets, but not as bad as I would have felt by giving up the rest of the people down in the Sanctuary so easily.

"I'm sure they do know it," I said, trying to comfort her.

"Are you done with your food?" she asked, eyeing the slop I left behind.

I pushed it to her, and she greedily ate my leftover portion.

Everyone was getting up to go out into the yard for an hour of exercise.

I looked to Dani for guidance.

She told me to go ahead; that she would help Bertha wash the dishes today.

That sounded a bit off to me, but I didn't question it.

I got up and moved towards the gray, dirt-filled square for fresh air. The chemical smell of the box soap in the laundry room was still stuck in my nose and clung to my uniform.

When I made it outside, I just stood there, taking in deep breaths that were only a step above breathing in the chemicals of the detergent.

I could smell sweat and desperation in the air.

There was nothing fresh about it, but it would have to do.

I slowly walked in the loosely formed circle until it was time to be corralled back inside.

Rio was waiting in the cell when I entered.

She was turned towards the wall while sitting on her bed and playing pretend doll games with her hands. Each finger was a different doll, and she gave them voices as she made their sounds with her mouth.

It was excruciating yet compelling to watch.

Here she was, with no toys, no friends, no entertainment, but she was still resilient enough to play pretend and be content in her present situation.

"Hey, Rio," I greeted.

"Raya! Do you wanna pway dolls with me?" she returned.

"Of course, I wanna play dolls with you!" I answered, smiling big at her.

I then stooped down near her bed and offered up my fingers.

7:30 AM. Saturday.

I lay in my hard bunk bed that didn't deserve to be called a bed. It was more like a hard cot with a raggedy thin blanket.

The smells that wafted through M block were horrendous. It was just tangent body odors everywhere you turned.

Fortunately, my cell smelled mostly of box detergent, compliments of laundry duty. Rio was practically still a baby and didn't have a ripe smell like all the other women.

The same routine as every other day began.

The banging of batons, the bright lights, people shuffling towards the bars of their cell.

My body instinctively rebelled.

It was the Sabbath, the day of rest.

Why aren't we resting?

Rio waved me to hurry before the doors opened.

Slothfulness equaled a demerit.

I got up and dragged myself through it, finally standing by the bars, waiting to be released for work.

Rio squeaked a small goodbye when the doors opened, and I walked with lead feet towards the laundry line.

I stood behind Dani, low in spirit.

It felt wickedly wrong to profane the Sabbath.

"Hey," Dani insisted, "You'll get used to it."

Then she turned around.

To everyone's shock and horror, Karen showed up to lead us to the Laundry Center.

All heads immediately bowed to the floor.

We began walking in silence in a straight line down the long gray hallway.

The older woman in front of Dani started to sway like she was getting dizzy. She tried to correct herself but stumbled backward into Dani. Dani had to step out of the line in order to bear the woman's weight as she fell back into her.

As she stepped out, her gray, worn-out shoe grazed against one of Karen's shiny black boots, causing a dull gray smudge to appear.

"Oh…that's a demerit for you, girl!" she loudly called out, grabbing Dani by her collar.

The faint woman had regained her footing and managed to straighten up in panic.

Karen pulled out a device that looked like a smartphone. She typed into it, and it notified her that prisoner M117 now had a total of four demerits.

"It's two days in the Chute for you," she confirmed aloud.

Guide appeared coming from the opposite side of the hallway, and Karen told her to escort the rest of us to work because she needed to take a delinquent to the Chute.

Guide nodded her chin towards her, then turned to take us further down the hall.

"No! Please! I didn't mean to…it was an accident. It was her fault!" screamed Dani, pointing back at the woman who had fallen into her.

She tried to squirm and pull away from Karen, but the soldier twisted her fist, gripping Dani's uniform tighter.

"That's another demerit! I can do this all day...try me!" the soldier retorted.

Dani screamed louder, "NOOO! PLEASE....IT WASN'T MY FAULT! NOOO!"

"That's another one! Let's see if you can handle four days in the Chute!" Karen maniacally spat out.

Dani suddenly went limp, and Karen had to drag her down the long hallway by her collar.

We took a right towards Laundry, and Karen and Dani disappeared from our sight.

My heart was beating so fast in my ears that I couldn't focus on anything but Dani's limp body floating down the gray floor, headed toward her worst fear.

After Guide let us in, we got to work.

My brain eventually calmed down, but my eyes kept searching for the missing member in our laundry room waltz.

Eleven

---◆---

Solo

I BARELY RECOGNIZED MYSELF when I looked in the mirror.

My eyes resembled a raccoon's since I was spending countless hours between building a digital model of the TRP and sitting with Juda and Ryan. Ryan hadn't left Juda's side in a week.

Ms. Lynn would bring him a tray of food every afternoon, but he wouldn't touch it.

I usually ended up eating it so Ms. Lynn wouldn't get offended over him wasting her good food.

I splashed water on my face to fully wake myself up.

It was almost time for the Shabbat lesson.

I walked up the metal staircase to the community room on the second level and found an empty seat between James and Gabriel. We didn't have much conversation before Elijah opened the service up in prayer and the reading from the Law.

The lesson was reasonably short and somber. It concerned perseverance in times of unknown outcomes. It was timely and gave me a renewed sense of hope for my cousins and all the lost people the Syndicate had conspiratorially kidnapped.

After the lesson, I saw Ryan come down the stairs and enter the massive room filled with people and their noises.

He got in line to get food.

I was glad to see that he finally left Juda's sick room, and I got in line behind him.

"Shabbat shalom[1]," I greeted him.

"Shabbat Shalawam[2]," he returned.

After we received our trays that contained a warm bowl of soup, rolls, and salad, we sat down at a table closest to the exit.

After Ryan slurped his first bite of the vegetable soup, he moaned ecstatically.

"This is the best soup I've ever had. How did they keep it so warm?" he asked and moaned again.

"I built an industrial-sized thermos when I was fifteen," I answered, proud that it actually worked. "Uncle Zeke

---

1. Hebraic greeting for a peaceful Sabbath

2. Hebraic greeting for a peaceful Sabbath- a variation

thought it would be put to good use down here...eventually."

He nodded his head and continued eating.

I tried to eat my soup, but my stomach was in knots, and I couldn't articulate why.

Something was wrong.

I could feel it.

I opened my phablet and read through Raya's transcripts. I couldn't make much sense of the last thing listed, but someone was getting reprimanded. As far as I could tell, it wasn't Raya, and that was hours ago.

She's been pretty quiet since.

Why do I feel this way?

"Um, I'm leaving tomorrow. I just thought you should know," Ryan randomly stated in between bites of his food.

"You can't leave. What do you mean...leave? This isn't a hotel you can just check out of," I melodramatically shot back.

He looked at me seriously and said, "It's been a week, okay. Juda isn't waking up, and Raya is still out there dealing with god-knows-what. I can't stay here. Maybe it's okay for *you* to sit on your hands and do nothing, but I need to do something, even if I gotta do it alone."

That stung.

"For your information, I am doing something...more than you actually. I've made a partial digital blueprint of the TRP based on Raya's conversations. Once it's complete, we'll know how to infiltrate it and rescue everyone. I've already put together a special team. We just need to wa—" Ryan didn't let me finish my sentence.

"You can wait. I'm not waiting. I just wanted you to know I'm leaving first thing in the morning. I figured I owed you that much," he interrupted.

"What's your deal, man? What's your fascination with my cousin, anyway? Nobody's asking you to be a hero. Just a few days ago, you were all like 'let's wait for Juda,' and now you're saying you can't wait for Juda. What are you doing?" I threw at him.

He looked at me, and I could see in his eyes that he was trying to find the right words.

"Raya trusted me when none of y'all would. She saw good in me. Honestly, she reminds me of my sister, Dakota," he tried to explain. "I would want someone to help her if I couldn't..."

"Fine, man, whatever. Go if you feel like you need to, but I still don't think it's a good idea for you to leave just yet. You have no backup...if they catch you, your fate will be worse than hers. You're a traitor," I responded, finally realizing why my stomach was in knots.

At the mention of the word 'traitor,' Ryan winced and stopped talking.

"Look, I'll see what I can do to help you, but once you leave...you're on your own," I ended.

He nodded his head and immediately got up to get seconds. I was sure he wanted to savor any last remnant of a home-cooked meal because he wasn't likely to get any more any time soon.

I forced myself to finish my meal, then checked the time.

The sun had set a while ago, so I returned my tray to Lillian, who was working in the kitchen with Ms. Lynn again.

They got along so well that Lillian was usually seen stuck by her side. They were often seen cackling about something or another.

I shuffled towards the stairwell and went up to my Lookout to see what I could conjure up for Ryan.

The place Raya was in sounded horrendous, and I hated that she even ended up there in the first place. If I knew how to get her out, I would be leaving with Ryan, but I felt it was irresponsible to go up against something that we didn't know the full weight of yet.

I checked the information transcribed from Raya and started to add to my blueprint.

30.422159, -88.821692

Ocean Springs, MS

Transcendent Reculturing Program

Program Director - Dr. Agatha Rainer, former professor of Sociology, PhD, fifteen years experience. Prior felonies: Hate Crime, one count Conspiracy Against Rights, two counts Deprivation of Rights Under Color of Law; expunged and sealed record.

Twenty-six blocks, A-Z.

A-M Female.

N-Z Male.

Electronic V-Groove slide gate/entrance.

Barracks - Twenty cells below, twenty above, tables and stools in the middle of the corridor, bolted to the floor.

Chute- torture chamber, a few stories high, middle of compound

Raya - M block

Miles of fencing, floodlights on every post, barbed wire, lookout towers with soldiers every twenty feet.

Swampland and trees beyond the fence.
Too many people to count…

Raya's words were like a math equation in my head.

I worked out the layout based on deduction and reason.

Eighty people per block. Twenty-six blocks. Equals at least 2,080 people if there was no overcrowding.

I guesstimated each block to be roughly 2,400 square feet each if there were ten cells on each side, up and down.

The block buildings had to wrap around like a linear U, with the yard butting against the fencing on the outer rim of the layout.

I knew there had to be work-related stations within the belly of the compound because no one ever saw other blocks from the inside. The hallways and corridors undoubtedly connected the workstations with certain blocks.

They had to have an intricate ventilation system, maybe even a basement utility for the HVAC system.

I need more information…I need more time.

I pushed the digital blueprint over from my main screen to the monitor next to me and began hacking into various government sites to build Ryan a new identity.

I scoured through Vital Statistics and the Social Security Administration, then moved on to the Department of

State. I pulled a tiny credit card chip out of my junk pile and began downloading his new persona onto it.

By the time I finished perfecting the placement of the chip and reprinting the passport over and over to ensure there were no flaws, it was 8 AM, and Ryan was strolling into my space.

"Hey," he nonchalantly greeted.

I turned around and gave him a tired, expressionless nod.

He was carrying a black backpack and eating a pastry from Ms. Lynn.

It also looked like he made a poor attempt at giving himself a haircut.

I snickered under my breath at his new style.

His curly bang was bluntly cut across his hairline, which made him resemble a 90s boy band member.

Well, at least the look would definitely highlight his new name.

I handed him my final product of a passport, fresh off the press, and he smirked at it.

"This looks just like the real thing," he beamed.

"Well, I am a genius...if you hadn't figured that out by now," I countered.

He opened the passport and immediately frowned his face up.

"Cornelius Smithers? Are you serious?" he scolded.

"Hey…I did what I could last minute, my guy," I responded while swiveling back to face the monitors, smiling deeply to myself.

His new name was a little going away present I had concocted, and I was more than proud of it.

We then discussed everything I had learned about the TRP, and I showed him my partially constructed layout.

He listened intently but did not share any of his plans.

I handed him the TRP coordinates on a slim strip of paper, and he stuffed it in his right front pocket.

Afterward, we walked down to the vault, and I gifted him a .38 caliber pistol with a few boxes of ammo, which he zipped up in his backpack.

Before we left the vault, the glass casement caught my eye.

Uncle Zeke's cryptic journals taunted me.

They were like calculations I couldn't solve, and that unnerved me.

The prominent red and green buttons on the wall behind the journals leered at me, begging to be pushed, but I hadn't figured out what purpose they served, and I was too apprehensive to find out the hard way.

We left the vault, and I locked it behind us.

"Thanks, man. I really appreciate everything. I hope we meet again, in this life or the next," Ryan said solemnly.

He turned and left as abruptly as he had come, and I watched him walk quickly down the exit tunnel and round the corner, out of my sight.

Afterward, I wandered back into the Lookout and watched the cameras.

I saw Ryan go out of the hatch and traipse away through the woods.

I yawned, shut everything down, locked the door behind me, and headed to bed.

TWELVE

ANGEL

"I'LL MEET YOU THERE in two hours," I announced to Jeremiah and Ava.

I put my overnight bag across my shoulder and moved for their apartment door.

I tried to stifle it by covering my mouth, but I coughed before I reached the door.

"You need to let me look you over, sis. Your cough is getting worse," Ava said as she shifted towards me to feel my forehead.

I dodged her hand and explained, "I'm fine, thank you. I'm just a little tired from all the travel."

She put her hand down in defeat.

As a doctor, the one thing Ava understood, if nothing else, was that some people wouldn't seek medical attention until just before it was too late.

"Most High willing, I will see y'all soon," I concluded, walking out the door to my ancient black pickup truck.

I decided to take the longer route of I-45 N since it would only account for one hour of travel, and I could avoid the tolls.

Then I would wait in the forest for the others.

I relished the freedom of the drive.

I rolled the windows down halfway and deeply breathed in the crisp air. Without Ava's watchful eyes judging me for it, I coughed at my leisure.

My chest felt full of pressure, and I could hear myself wheezing whenever I exhaled, but I didn't have time for sickness.

After this, I could go home, and that's the only thing I wanted more than my next meal, next day, next breath.

When I finally pulled off the interstate, I entered the narrow roadway towards the beginning of the Lone Star Hiking Trail.

I put my overnight bag across my shoulders like a hiking pack and began walking the trail, using my compass to navigate. I continued for some time, veering off to the right of the much-used path.

I walked through thick brush and brambles before locating a stream of brackish-looking water. I followed it north for some time, then stopped in a clearing and waited.

I put my pack down and pulled out my head covering. This was the perfect spot and time to pray.

Most holy and high Power in heaven, Father, I come before You to glorify Your presence. You, and You alone, are worthy to be praised. Thank You, Father, for all that You have done and all that You will do. I earnestly pray that You gather Your people unto You in a safe place and that all things come to pass as it is Your will to do so. Please provide traveling mercy to all who seek Your comfort and protection, Father. In all these things, I pray in Your son's righteous and holy name, Yashaya Hamashiach[1], Amen.

After I prayed, I sat there and took in the beautiful scenery and weather.

I could hear birds singing to one another and the brook gurgling tranquilly nearby.

It was such a peaceful, quiet place.

It almost made me forget what the world was like outside of these woods.

Suddenly, I heard boots stepping onto stagnant leaves somewhere off behind me.

I got up quickly to see who was approaching.

It was almost time, but I could never be too careful.

---

1. Hebraic name of Jesus the Messiah or Jesus Christ

The small caliber pistol was tucked into the back waistband of my wide-legged pants, and I felt for the safety of it.

When my eyes trained on the intruders, I immediately recognized Jeremiah and Ava. They had a small congregation with them, maybe thirty to forty people. Another group trekked in from the east. That group looked even more significant, with perhaps sixty or seventy people.

I smiled to the heavens.

Thank you, Father.

"Is this everyone?" I asked once they all made it relatively close.

"Yes, there's about a hundred and twenty of us, praise the Most High," Jeremiah answered.

I nodded in agreement, "Praise Him, indeed. We have another ten minutes or so to reach the actual location, and then we can descend. Please follow me."

Jeremiah called out to the group, preparing them to be on the move again.

We walked deeper into the forest until we happened upon a fully bloomed Franklin tree.

I stood before the tree, blocking my movements from the onlookers, and pulled the single white flower in the middle.

I heard the hatch door disengage, and I reached down and pulled the lever so that the entrance swiveled open. The lights down below immediately came on, illuminating the way down.

Jeremiah directed the crowd to climb down into the underground tunnel, and it took all of forty minutes for everyone to fully descend.

After the entire group was herded into the narrow passageway, I made sure no one else was in the area before I went down myself.

I hated this part.

I did not care to be underground.

I needed sunshine and grass and car rides and...freedom.

But out of all these things, being in or around water was my actual love language. The ultimate thrill was the open ocean breeze and the swaying of a fast-moving ship. It's one of the reasons why I joined the Navy shortly after graduating high school.

When I married my high school sweetheart, we were dead broke. Eating noodles out of a cup every night and constantly getting our lights and water shut off due to non-payment wasn't exactly an ideal life, especially starting out.

My husband wanted to attend college but needed money, so I joined the service. It was the quickest way to secure his tuition, and I could go to college online after he completed his degree.

I loved all things water, so it was a no-brainer.

For the short time I was enlisted, the skillset it provided gave me a militaristic mindset, and I used that to my full advantage now.

Jumping to the bottom of the tunnel, I maneuvered past the group to the front. The automatic lights illuminated the way to the heart of the bunker.

"I'm sorry to have to do this to you, but it will be a three-mile walk to where we need to be. Please follow me," I coughed out.

It took a while for everyone to make it to the stairwell that led down to their new home, but there were things to see along the way.

I pointed out the library to our left and the laundry room to our right. I explained the vault and what it housed.

Once we reached the stairs, I pointed further down the tunnel instead of descending the steps immediately. I explained how that corridor was set up, leading out to the exit tunnel, "Further down, you will find a hydroponics room, a fitness center, a playground, and the security lookout."

We then took the short steps to the community room, and everyone dropped their luggage and bags.

I showed Jeremiah the blueprints and asked that he make the room assignments as he and Ava saw fit.

I needed to sit down.

My body was betraying me, and I could feel the heat radiating from my skin.

It was more than the three-mile trek that reduced me to weakness.

Ava saw that I was tired and flushed, so she approached.

"I think you may have bronchitis, sis. It would be best if you let me check you," she insisted.

I didn't fight her.

I couldn't.

She pulled out a stethoscope from her backpack and asked me to breathe deeply after she donned it.

I complied.

She checked several times at various locations on my chest and back. I was sure she heard the rattling sounds of mucus choking my lungs. I knew it was there but kept telling myself to move past it...to push forward.

I desperately needed to get home, and I didn't want to stay down here more than a few days to help them set up.

"This has moved past bronchitis. You have pneumonia. We will have to quarantine you from the rest of the body. Where should we take you?" she asked earnestly.

"I can't stay here," I coughed. "I have other places to be and a schedule to keep."

She shook her head.

"You won't make it much longer constantly going like this. You need rest. True rest. You can't leave until you are 100% better...doctor's orders," she commanded.

Through hacking coughs, I explained to her that a single pod was on the sixth level. It consisted of a storage room with a solitary bunk bed. I gathered no one would need it for a while, seeing how most people brought their own initial supplies.

I would quarantine there.

She took some rubbing alcohol out of her pack and washed her hands in it before following me down the stairs leading all the way to the bottom.

"I will see about getting you some medicinal teas going. There's a brother here who brought some healing herbs, and I'm sure that will help for now. I'll check on you in a bit," Ava said, watching me crawl into the bottom bunk, exhausted.

I closed my eyes, but the pain in my body would not subside.

The last thought on my mind before debilitating fatigue overtook me was of the sea, glistening in the sun, blue and ripe with its warm, salty smell.

Thirteen

Raya

7:30 AM. Sunday.

I opened my heavy eyes and blinked at the gray wall I faced in my gray cell.

My entire outlook was starting to fade into the same shade of misery, and I was sure I had a heavy coat of gray crust layering the top of my unwashed skin.

It had been a week, and no one had come for me.

No one cared.

It was just as well because I was right where I deserved to be.

The banging of the batons, the bright lights, the morning insults.

Nothing was new but the day.

Rio tugged on my thin blanket as I stared at the concrete, hugging myself in self-pity.

"Good mowning, Raya," she whispered. "It's wash day. Come on, sweepyhead."

I turned over and looked down at the living baby doll in my cell.

She smiled up at me and waved me down.

I couldn't do anything but oblige.

Her little chubby cheeks and oversized brown eyes could coerce me into doing just about anything.

"Wash day?" I repeated.

She nodded her head.

We stood at the bars, as always, anticipating being released. When the doors chimed and slid open, the women started lining up in numerical, single-file order instead of everyone lining up to go to their workstations. The line wrapped around the lower level of cells.

I followed Rio to our spot, and we waited.

Dark Shades and Guide appeared from one of the hallways, and they immediately started leading us down the long, straight corridor further inwards.

Instead of my usual right turn to Laundry, we kept straight...the same direction Dani was drug away in just yesterday.

We walked a few silent moments, then took a left down an unmarked gray side passage. On the left and right sides of the hallway were entrances marked 'Showers, Female'.

The women before me started filing into them, six at a time.

I couldn't see inside from where I stood, but when it was our turn to enter, there were rough gray towels, tiny bars of white soap, and a plastic set of thin shower shoes waiting on shelves bolted to the walls.

The ladies grabbed one set each and entered the open yet partitioned stalls.

I took a set down for Rio and one for myself.

I bent down and asked Rio, "Do you need any help?"

She nodded, "The buttons."

I helped her disrobe and put the shower shoes on her tiny feet.

The shoes were like flip-flops that weren't worthy of being called anything shoe-related.

Rio then went into a stall to shower all by herself.

I found an empty stall, quickly got out of my week-old clothes, and discarded them in the bin marked for Laundry.

The entire room smelled of mildew, and a case of athlete's foot would surely await if a barefoot accidentally touched the soggy floor.

The shower only had one spigot, but instead of my expectations of straight icy, cold water, it was lukewarm, like pool water that had been marinating in the afternoon sun.

If I had ever taken a shower for granted before, this one humbled me.

It was like finally getting a cool glass of water on a hot summer day or biting into a ripe, juicy piece of fruit when something was needed to satisfy a sweet tooth.

I wasn't told how long they allowed us to be in there, so I rushed to clean myself and wash my low, almost faded hair. They had not provided us with wash clothes, so I used my short nails, along with the tiny piece of soap, to scrape and dig at the top layer of filth and rough skin that was callused by the heat blisters.

I made good time because the batons started banging on the walls as I rinsed off, signaling us to exit.

I wrapped the scratchy towel around myself and dried off as fast as possible before exiting the stall.

There were no toiletries granted...no lotions, butters, or deodorants.

My skin instantly ashed up from the thirst for soft water and products.

On the bench, bolted to the floor right outside the showers, lay six fresh sets of clothes with our three cell numbers marked.

I picked up my set and Rio's set, and after dressing myself, I helped her put on her clothes, rolling up the sleeves and pant legs several times until they fit somewhat.

We lined back up, walked out a separate doorway, back into the main hall, and waited patiently until our entire block had showered.

After Guide and Dark Shades were satisfied with our progress, they had us break out into our work lines.

I knew it was too good to be true.

There was no day of rest here.

Most of the women remained in one primary line, while I went to Laundry with the other three laundry workers in a separate line.

Rio was the only little one at the very back of the main line.

I wanted to ask one of the ladies where they were going, but I glanced up and saw cameras along the entire corridor that deterred me from opening my mouth. Maybe at dinner, I could strike up a conversation with someone.

We were corralled back down the hallway by Guide, and my group veered to the left while the main group went right, with Rio being taken by Dark Shades straight through the block and out to the yard, towards the Intake Center.

It never occurred to me to ask Rio where she went every day, but I would rectify that tonight.

I guessed we only lost about two hours of work time while M block showered. That would be the full extent of our weekly amount of rest.

A fresh mountain of uniforms and undergarments awaited us when we arrived.

The same rigmarole commenced after we were locked in for the next six hours.

Some of the women conversed in their unique, secretive way, but there was no one for me to communicate with or ask my questions and be taken seriously, anyway.

With Dani gone, there was a gaping void, and we had to labor extra hard to keep up with the demands of our work.

Three more days, and she could return.

From the way she spoke about the Chute, I knew it was unlikely that she would come back whole, but at least she would be out.

She would have to strive to become at least a piece of her former self.

I was starting to believe that to be true of all of us.

After the daily monotonous labor, we were released to dinner.

I saw Rio sitting alone near the mess counter, but Dark Shades stood uncomfortably close to her. I wanted to join

Rio, but I didn't trust to ask her about her day near any of the guards, so I found a seat closer to our cell.

I sat next to a stern-looking woman with an afro puff ponytail.

She didn't seem fazed by my presence, so I tried to strike up a conversation.

"Hi. I'm Raya," I said casually.

"Hey, Raya, I'm trying to eat in peace. Do you mind? The guards are always watching, and I got two demerits as it is," she returned, then went back to eating the mystery meal swimming in a white gravy.

I poked at my food but decided today was the day to eat the entire meal.

Hearing Dani's warning in my head, I slowly ate half, offering the rest to Afro Puff, but she declined. I drank half of my bottled water and held onto the rest for the next morning.

After discarding my tray, I noticed Dark Shades was still lurking around Rio, but it seemed more for protection than anything sinister.

I still didn't get it.

Dark Shades made sure she called us every byword under the sun as often as she could. Although she was no Karen, she was verbally abusive, and I witnessed her giving out demerits during my short stay here. I knew for a fact that she had no qualms with disciplining small children.

Why would she want to protect Rio, then?

I trudged outside.

I didn't want to walk in a circle like a farm animal stuck in limbo, but what else could I do?

There were no books, no call to prayer, no family, no fun, no friends. Just mindless, hard labor with no end in sight.

After the exercise hour was up, we were ushered back into our cells for the night. Approaching mine, I found Rio curled up on her bunk, whimpering.

When she heard me coming, she quickly asked for help to rewash her new outfit.

She had soiled herself.

"What's going on, Rio? Is someone hurting you or scaring you? You can tell me," I calmly asked while I took off her uniform and cleaned her up.

I was trying to sound composed, but my emotions were running high at the thought of anyone purposely abusing the child.

She looked up at me from under her blanket and said, "They show us scawy stuff at schoow, and I don't wanna be awone."

"What do you mean...'scary stuff'? Stuff like what?" I continued to probe.

"Demons," she answered.

I didn't want to push her too hard on that subject, so I asked her what other things she learned at school.

As I rubbed the filth from her uniform, she told me all about the recitations they had to say every day, even if they didn't want to, and about the strange books that were read to them. They were not teaching them how to read or write.

They just had to sit and listen and repeat.

"You know that a demon can't get you if you trust and believe in the Most High, right?" I tried to comfort her.

She nodded, "I know, but the pictures are scawy. They show us evawyday."

I was almost done with her clothes when I told her that we could hold hands and say a quick prayer for protection when they cut the lights out.

She looked worried and said, "We can't. We get in trawble."

I told her it would be really quick, and no one would see, but she was too afraid.

"Okay, no worries. I'll say a prayer silently for you then, okay? You can't get in trouble for something they can't hear," I said, smiling down at her.

She looked at me blankly and rolled over in her bunk as if she had no more room to believe in fairytales.

7:30 AM. Tuesday.

I floated through the morning routine as if I was having an out-of-body experience.

The monotony of it all was mentally wearing me thin, and I had long since checked out.

I barely knew what day it was, and the only thing keeping me afloat was the thought of Dani showing back up tomorrow.

I was already listing topics we could discuss to bring her mind back to lucidness...her family, her school, her church, her good memories.

While Karen walked us to the Laundry Center, she seemed to be in an extra-giving mood.

She gave two of the ladies a demerit each for not walking fast enough down the hall.

After letting us in, we got to work as rapidly as possible, knowing that she would be on camera duty today and would be looking for a reason, any reason, to punish.

No one said a word, not even when the door opened and a new person was escorted in.

I happened to be at the washing machines, shoving in the foul-smelling clothes, when the new girl's presence caught my attention.

I looked over at her and did a double-take.

She was skinnier than I remembered, and her hair was styled much differently, but it was Shiri.

I couldn't believe my eyes.

My best friend had materialized right in front of me, and I couldn't do a thing to express my joy at the sight of her.

I had to keep feeding clothes into the machines.

She took one look at me and almost ran at me for an embrace. I quickly whispered under my breath for her to stop and nodded to the cameras with my chin ever so slightly.

She took the hint and looked for guidance on what to do next.

She followed my eyes to the mountain of stinky uniforms, then to the machines I currently loaded. She comprehended right away and started picking up clothes without saying a word. When it was time to rotate, I pointed slyly to the folding tables without lifting my arm.

She understood and moved.

Shiri watched me fold a few uniforms while she fiddled with hers to make it seem like she was inspecting them. She then started to fold, catching on quickly. We went on like this until it was time to rotate to the dryers. When I walked over, she followed suit.

We did this for hours, happy to breathe the same air as each other again.

I couldn't wait for this shift to end, and we could sit down and actually talk.

We just had to make it past Karen's need to torment someone.

After several rotations, we found ourselves back at the folding table, and I noticed Shiri looking over at the rules poster and then down at the underwear in her hand that sported a massive hole in the waistband. She continued to fold it and was about to move on when I seized it before she could cover it up with another pair. I marched it over to the door, banged on it twice, and waited for a guard to come get the damaged article. I then quickly returned to my workstation and got back to work.

She looked at me, bewildered.

I looked back at her, and we had a face-off.

My face said, 'Don't challenge me...I did it to protect you'.

Then hers read, 'Fine, whatever, but you gonna have to explain that one later'.

It was like we hadn't even been apart for the past four months.

The eight-hour shift felt like an eternity, but it finally ended, and we were allowed to leave.

As the next group of five passed us in the hallway, I caught a glimpse of their block letter, which was J.

I worked it out in my head.

So M block worked the first shift, J worked the second, and H worked the third, and it was always just five women at a time.

We made it to M block unscathed by Karen, picked up our trays of food, and found two empty seats next to each other. We sat with our knees touching, knowing that would be the closest thing to a hug we would be allowed.

"Shiri, praise the Most High you are alive," I started, eating and smiling.

I was too ecstatic to see her, that is, until I saw the number attached to the front of her uniform...*M117*.

That was Dani's number.

"Where is she?" I blurted out a little too aggressively.

"Where is who?" she defensively answered.

"Dani...you have on her uniform. She went to the Chute three days ago. She's supposed to come back tomorrow," I answered quickly.

"Raya, I don't know anyone named Dani. Do you know how huge this place is?" she answered sincerely.

She took a bite of her food and continued, "Besides, they move people all the time. This is my third move. You may never see her again."

I looked at my tray of weirdly shaped mush covered in brown gravy before continuing to eat.

She was probably right, and I would have to come to terms with never seeing Dani again.

"Where have you been? Tell me more about this place," I asked, trying to move past that fact.

"Well, I started on K block with my mom, and we both worked as cleaners for the Intake Center and the officers' barracks. Then, when they figured out our relation a few weeks in, they moved me to D block, and I've been working in the kitchen ever since. I help make the gravies," she laughed, picking some up onto her spork and letting it slide back down to the tray with a loud plop.

I wrinkled my nose at it.

"Don't give me that look. If you only knew exactly what you were eating, you would be thanking me for the gravy," she quipped.

I looked at her questioning.

"No, don't worry, it's kosher. We take care to throw all the pork and other abominations away in special bags so the guards don't find out. It's just...mostly grade F meat, so it's practically rotten and diseased. They force us to cook it, but we use as little as possible to get by. The gravy is to hide the fact that you aren't even eating that much meat," she answered.

I looked at my tray again but with a renewed sense of appreciation that they were using inmates, who still cared, to cook the food.

"Oh! Naomi is in the D block," she remembered suddenly.

"That's good to know...she was at least with someone else she knew," I reasoned, knowing that Naomi was also suffering harshly from Juda's death.

Shiri shook her head sadly before stating, "No. Naomi is all alone...in her mind. She hasn't acknowledged my existence since she arrived over a week ago. She started turning people in for frivolous things, too. It's like sleeping with the enemy. You have to keep one eye open around her. She isn't the Naomi we once knew, and I'm actually glad they moved me away from her."

My heart sank for Naomi.

"What about her parents? Did they make it here?" I asked, eagerly trying to process as much information as possible.

We didn't have much time to catch up, and I would have to wait twenty-four more hours to talk with Shiri freely again.

She nodded but looked forlorn about it.

"From what I heard, her mom released herself, and when her dad found out, he tried to escape. They executed him the next day," she explained.

"Does Naomi know any of that?" I asked.

She nodded her head again.

Naomi lost everyone she ever loved.

I was about to ask Shiri exactly what 'released herself' meant when we were interrupted by Dark Shades.

She told us dinner time was up and to get moving out into the yard.

We both discarded our trays, moved towards the yard's open doorway, and walked in the despairing circle for an hour. Shiri walked slightly in front of me to avoid calling any unwanted attention to our friendship.

We would be separated if anyone found out.

After the walk, we went to our respective cells for lights out.

As I entered, I had a million questions swimming in my head when I heard Rio sniffling.

"What's the matter, little sis?"

"I wanna go home," she cried out.

I wanted to hug her and rock her to comfort her.

She shouldn't be here.

I spoke soft words to her and stroked her hair occasionally when not many people were looking.

I couldn't embrace her.

It wasn't allowed.

We could both get a demerit.

I despised this gray pit of affliction.

Miss called it a program, but it wasn't a program at all...it was nothing more than a prison.

Four-year-olds did not belong in prison, and I was getting angrier by the second.

Fourteen

Solo

I SAT IN THE white fold-out chair placed next to Juda's bed in the Infirmary. The lights were dimmed, but I could see perfectly well that my cousin was still motionless and inert.

There was rampant silence permeating the air except for Juda's raspy exhales. I would have thought he was faintly snoring if I hadn't known any better.

I should have been glad for that precious sound, but it was well over a week, and the only change in Juda was the swelling of his limbs.

Mira said it was to be expected with the constant administering of saline fluids, but Juda looked like a homemade water balloon crafted from a latex glove.

Adina was due back any moment with a concoction to help Juda's kidneys and liver detox the poison still circulating in his body.

She would also bring him his daily dose of Willow tea.

I hung my head in a silent prayer for his recovery and that the Most High's will be done in all things.

Then Juda and I had a one-sided conversation.

"I never realized how much I needed you, man. Raya, too. I got nobody to talk to, for real, and no one to laugh with. Everything's been going okay down here, I guess, but it feels like something's missing...y'all are missed. I found out some stuff from Raya...Shiri is with her now. Praise the Father. Naomi isn't doing so well, though. I wish we could go get them, but I just don't know how yet. We got a special team together that's willing and able, but there is no slam-dunk plan. We got Big Man and Farmer John, of course, then James, Hector, that new kid, Jashawn, and an older guy, Charles. I was hoping to recruit more people than that, but I'm grateful," I rambled.

I paused and waited as if Juda were going to respond, but he never did.

I continued and told Juda all about the clogged water filtration system that I had to fix and my latest idea for a mission simulator in the training room. I told him all the things he wouldn't have had the time to hear before but had no choice except to partake in now.

Adina returned with a tray in hand.

She offered a small smile and went to the other side of Juda's bed to administer his tea and medicine. She pretended she wasn't eavesdropping, but I could tell she had heard most of what I said.

I didn't care.

I kept talking to him about nothing in particular, hoping he had tuned in to my voice.

Anything to strengthen his mind.

No one knew if or when he would wake up, and even though he could breathe independently, he showed no other signs of life.

"You know...I talk to him, too, sometimes. With all my heart, I believe he can hear us, and we need to keep talking. We only talk to people who matter, and he matters," Adina mentioned in my direction while putting the liquids into Juda's feeding tube.

I nodded and watched silently for a moment, not wanting to bother her, but that nagging question leaked out of my mouth again.

The same question Adina had answered a thousand times, at least.

"Do you think he will wake up soon?" I asked, hoping for a different answer this time.

She sighed deeply before responding, "There's no way to tell. I'm sorry, Solo. Just keep praying for him, okay?"

I stared at my blue and white tennis shoes, focusing on the knot in one of the strings that I couldn't seem to pick out.

Juda was like that knot.

I couldn't figure out how to make it right...I couldn't undo it.

There was no equation for me to work out or system to invent that would jolt him awake.

He was in the Most High's hands, and I just needed to stay out of His way.

I got up and shuffled out of the room, leaving Adina to her unrewarded work.

There was nowhere else to go that I would be productive, so I went to my Lookout and mindlessly checked the security feeds, as if I were watching TV.

My thoughts were in a tangle, still trying to grasp the fact that Raya had been kidnapped, Juda was practically a vegetable, and I was alone, trapped in my own worthlessness.

I began to ponder what my purpose was in all of this.

Maybe it was up to me to liberate Raya and the thousands of others from the TRP.

There was no way Ryan could be relied upon... I was almost certain that he was going to get himself killed if he hadn't already.

Raya was no count, either.

She didn't seem too focused on escaping, and I was afraid her spirit was steadily being bent until someday, maybe soon, it would finally snap into pieces. I needed to get to her before that could happen.

I knew where the TRP was, but I had an incomplete diagram.

Father, what should I do?

I turned on Raya's transcripts instead of picking up the headphones to listen.

I couldn't bear to hear the constant dejection in her voice, so instead of reading anything she had to say, I thought about all my absent loved ones. Then, an image of my mother, who was still alive and well, popped into my head.

I should call her.

It had been three months since I last spoke to her when Raya suggested I reach out.

I wanted to feel like everything was normal, at least for a moment. My mother could provide that for me.

Ignoring the transcripts altogether, I pulled out my phablet and opened the special app I created to talk to my mom safely.

I had to put in a few passcodes before it opened up for me, but once it opened, I paused in confusion when the tag on the corner of the screen gave me the date of my last usage:

Sunday, October 8th, 2028. 4:15 AM.

That was the day Raya was taken, when I found Drea snooping around the Lookout.

I was confused because I hadn't opened the app since July.

Maybe Drea had been tampering with more of my stuff before she was caught.

Not possible...my phablet is always on me.

I rubbed my temples, trying to release the sudden tension headache that had crept up on me when I heard a light rapping at my door.

"Come in," I responded loudly.

To my surprise, it was Lillian and her weird little sister. No matter how hard I tried, I couldn't remember the girl's name. The sister was wearing a bright pink headwrap and in some kind of way, had it twisted into two pigtails.

"Lynn fixed you a bowl of vegetable stew, and I made some rolls," Lillian said, smiling at me sincerely while offering the tray. "We didn't see you at dinner, and she knows how much you love her stew, so she asked me to bring it to you."

"Thank you," I flatly said, not remotely interested in the bowl of steaming hot vegetables swimming in thick stock.

She wrinkled her brow at me and asked, "Are you okay? Is it Raya?"

I felt the tears welling up from deep within, and I tried to stuff them back down but couldn't hold them any longer.

Raya's name coming from someone else's mouth was enough to make me break.

I wailed, and Lillian rushed to put the tray down. Then she wrapped her arms around me in a tight embrace, and my face cradled into her shoulder.

I cried like a little kid who had just lost his best friend, and it was an embarrassingly loud shriek.

I didn't care.

Then I felt another, more petite person hugging my waist.

There was nothing I could do to push them away, nor did I want to.

I hoped Lillian hadn't taken my breakdown out of context. I had to let her know that Raya was still alive, and I was doing everything humanly possible to keep it that way, but before I could gather myself properly to speak, the strange girl's voice carried through the room.

"You shouldn't be so worried about Raya...I had a dream...she will be okay. You have to trust in the Most High," she said suddenly. "She's there for a reason. She survived the attack in the woods for a reason. I'm sorry about your other cousin, but you know...it could've easily been Raya lying there on her deathbed instead. She's still alive because she's got a purpose to fulfill. You need to know that."

"Maya, this might not be the best time to share stuff like that," Lillian seethed through a nervous smile. "Why don't you go check on Ya-el?"

Maya let me go and then quickly flew away, out of the room and down the stairs, leaving me to feel worse than I did starting off.

"I'm sorry about my sister. We are still working on...timing. I'll leave you to your stew. You need to eat something. It may help you feel better," Lillian anxiously concluded before exiting the room herself.

That one sentence replayed in my mind repeatedly until it became my personal torture.

It could've easily been Raya lying there on her deathbed instead.

That abnormal child was suggesting that Juda's fate had already been decided...he was going to die.

FIFTEEN

---◆---

ANGEL

"Uhhhhh..." I groaned. "My face feels like it's melting off. Make it stop..."

I laid in the bottom bunk, stretched out, waiting impatiently for the grip of sickness to let me go.

I was freezing, but sweat had soaked through my loose t-shirt and sweatpants. My chest felt like gobs of pudding were lodged in my lungs. It was dry and rough every time I coughed, and nothing was coming up or out. I didn't want to continue coughing because it burned the back of my throat and was incessant once it started.

I just wanted it to end.

Ava chuckled slightly while looking at her thermometer.

"Your fever has finally broken, and the humidifier will do wonders for your lungs. There's not much I can do about your face, though. You'll be happy to know that it's not melting off," she quipped.

"What day is it?" I whined, finally opening my eyes to question Ava.

I had completely lost count of the days and really needed to get back on my feet.

I had never been sick for this long.

"It's Tuesday," she answered, packing her medical supplies into a small pouch.

"Thanks, but I mean, what's the actual date?" I returned, hoping I had not lost too many days.

"Um, it's October 24th. Why? Where do you have to be so badly?" she questioned.

I groaned again, mad at my body for not keeping up with my mental expectations. My goal was to be on the road no later than October 15th.

My soul cried out to go home.

"I have a family that I need to get back to," I bluntly responded, careful not to give out too much information.

I wasn't sure if Ava could be trusted with my history or if anyone could, for that matter. I did not want to put her or them in more danger than they were already.

To honestly know me was hazardous, and I had to protect these people and my family at all costs.

I pushed myself up to a seated position and asked Ava how much longer she thought I needed to recover.

"It's hard to say at this point, but you have a touch of malnutrition, too, which I suspect has something to do with you rushing about the country, not taking proper care of yourself, hmmm?" she said, giving me the side-eye.

"Well, praise the Most High, y'all are stuffing me with soups and herbs and bread, then," I chuckled, then went into a coughing spell.

Ava handed me a glass of water, which I quickly accepted and downed within seconds.

"I hate this!" I grumbled after finishing the water, and the coughing died away.

"Well, you never know...this could be God's will for you to rest and get some weight back on those bones before you get back to your family. Just saying..." Ava stated while throwing up her hands in the air.

"Kan[1]. Maybe. It's just...I had all these grand plans, and the Holy Spirit keeps moving me in other directions. I'm trying to be obedient to that calling...for the protection of our people, but I miss my family beyond anything you can comprehend, Ava," I lamented, emotion building alongside the mucus in my throat.

"I get it, sis, but the Most High always rewards obedience, even if we don't understand the 'why' behind the

---

1. Hebraic word indicating agreement

'what' yet. I remember when Jeremiah first came into this understanding of who we are biblically and the purpose we actually serve. You have no idea how hard it was for me to submit to it. I mean, I'm a doctor...everything's facts, logic, and science for me, but when I finally opened up the Word[2] for myself and started studying...I saw that the facts, logic, and science were already there this whole time in our Creator's designs and ways. It was easier to submit to it then for myself. Before, we fought every other day about faith, food, and even clothes. It was exhausting, and I was honestly looking for a divorce attorney. But looking back on those growing pains, I see now that all of that struggle and strife had to happen in order for me to go seek for myself...for me to love the Most High, not because someone was telling me to...but because I wanted to. Sorry. I didn't mean to be so long-winded. I know you need your rest," she said, then laughed nervously.

She looked like she was about to head for the door from where she sat in the tiny chair near the desk.

Before she could bolt for the exit, I replied, "No, I get it, sis. Truly, thank you for your testimony. It's good to be reminded and encouraged to stay the course. I know the Father has greater plans for all of us, and me getting to be

2. Bible

with my family again will be that much sweeter when it does happen."

I offered her a grateful smile before laying back down.

"I'll check on you again in a bit and bring you some dinner. Charlene is making something with sweet potatoes and green beans," she said, with a touch of humor in her voice, then she gave me a knowing look.

"Tell Charlene her efforts are appreciated," I replied, managing a short giggle without coughing again.

Sixteen

- ❦ -

Raya

I LOOK BACK, AND the fence surrounding the gray prison is waning. The buildings look ancient and are crumbling from the top all the way down to the bottom.

No one is in the yard, all the lights are out, and the sun is covered by gray clouds, making the place look even more dreary.

I stand in quicksand in the middle of the swampy lands outside the fence.

I can't contend with it, and slowly, I sink into the earth.

I hear something or someone gurgling in the distance.

I turn back to face the woods and see the figure of a frail woman, far away, sinking into the marshlands. Her consumption is much further along than mine, and she is choking on mud, fighting the land, trying to get out.

I try to get to her.

I want to help, but the more I stir, the quicker I'm pulled under. I can't make it to her in time, so I stop struggling and *watch as the woman's head disappears under the wet sand with the final pop of a soft air bubble.*

I stare at the spot, mesmerized by her disappearance.

Soon, I will join her.

7:30 AM. Wednesday.

Baton banging on the bars, Dark Shades announced, "Get up, vermin! Report to the yard for general assembly! I repeat, REPORT TO THE YARD FOR GENERAL ASSEMBLY."

I grumbled and hugged myself tighter in the top bunk. I could see my breath blowing out in a slow, frosted stream.

The temperature had plummeted recently, and I no longer had my ragged, papery blanket to offset the cold. Rio needed it more than me.

The material was so thin I could hear her fidgeting and whining in her bed, trying to get warm, and it was all I could do to help her.

I rolled out of the bed, leaping to the floor. I jogged in place for a few moments to jump-start my circulation. I knew I would be okay once I got into the steamy laundry room, but Dark Shades said we had to meet outside first for an impromptu assembly.

The weather was developing a wintry feel, and I wasn't trying to draw attention to myself because of a jittery reaction.

I would have to remain as still as possible.

I encouraged Rio to jog with me. She jumped right in and smiled up at me while we both internally warmed ourselves.

When it was time to step to the bars and wait to be released, we had both worked up enough heat to be grateful for the effort.

Dark Shades then ushered us outside like a herd of sheep into our designated section of the yard. Miss was standing on her portable raised platform and looking out to all of us from her podium like she was addressing filthy rags. Her facial expressions were just as cold as the wind that whipped around us. With her eyes glazed over, she seemed to try her hardest to see through us instead of looking directly at us. It was clear from her mannerisms, we were not people.

That suited me just fine because I wanted nothing to do with her unwelcome attention. That would most certainly wake up some cruel and humiliating inclination in her twisted mind...something I didn't want to witness or play a part in.

The warmth I had so desperately worked up just a few minutes ago dissipated quickly.

Looking down at my hands out of habit, I could see my flesh-toned nail beds changing into a deep purplish blue color.

The air arising from the nearby gulf waters put out a fresh breeze of frigid wind. I might as well have been wearing nothing but my underwear because the long-sleeved uniform was just as paper-thin as the raggedy blankets assigned to us.

I immediately started to shiver uncontrollably and noticed most of the M block inmates were doing the same. Though it was unspoken, we all impulsively moved a little closer to one another to gain some relief from the weather. The whole assembly of people became a tighter unit, and we were now considerably less spaced out.

This was not lost on Miss as she began her address, "If you all haven't realized it, it's now November 1st and the start of our winter season. Our gracious Commander has so thoughtfully gifted each and every one of you a present for your hard work and compliance to the Program. We've made it several weeks without any major incident, and this has not gone unnoticed—" she wagged her pointer finger at us like we were pets receiving a treat before continuing,

"—the Commander has rewarded you for this by securing coats for each of you. Isn't that exciting?"

She paused while plastering a black-hearted smirk on her face. She motioned to the guards who were standing just off the platform to bring the large brown boxes onto the stage.

While they dropped them at her feet, she turned back to us and instructed in her nice-nasty voice, "As always, ladies first, so we will start with A block. Line up and collect your allowance. Once you've come up to collect it, you are to report immediately to your workstations. We have quotas to meet, and this is by no means a free day."

The guards for A block started pushing the women forward into conformity. The haggard group shuffled towards Miss' stage but kept their eyes to the dirt. I had a clear view of the platform since M block was in the middle of all the other blocks, and Miss had situated herself to get as much exposure as possible.

The coats were a predictable shade of gray. They were not thick but looked substantially better than freezing to death.

The women walked in a straight line by the stage, underneath Miss as she continued to admonish us. They reached into the large box one by one, drawing out a coat each. A guard holding an AK-47 stood near the box to ensure no one took more than their share. As they trudged by us, I started to see one or two familiar faces from my church.

My heart fluttered with longing as they walked away.

No one took their eyes from the ground, and I couldn't call out to them, so instead, I said their names under my breath as they marched past.

"*Patricia. Wanda...*"

Then it was B block's turn.

On and on it went, and I whispered their names in acknowledgment.

When I saw Naomi pass by, she was almost unrecognizable. Her countenance had hardened, and that underlying boorish quality she had hidden for years was fully displayed. I could even see it in her gait.

When it got to G block, I saw a woman with the same modelesque bushy eyebrows and body build as Dani.

"*Shawna...*"

There were so many sisters that I didn't see, and I felt a deep pang of sorrow, thinking they must not have made it. As morbid as the thought was, I couldn't help but wonder where they were buried. I also wondered what had become of my mama. I did not have the imagination to lump her into the category with all the other missing ladies.

The procession took over an hour to reach M block. We were the last of the females, all trembling excessively from the long wait in the elements.

As Dark Shades pushed us into a straight line, Rio slipped in front of me and looked up for approval. I nodded at her once, without speaking, and then we moved towards the box. The coats were running out, and I had to reach deep to get one out for Rio.

After handing it to her, I put my hand back into the box for myself.

The guard with the AK-47 immediately pointed it at me.

"You must be deaf or something. Only one, rat!" the male soldier yelled at me.

"I don't have one, sir. I was helping this little girl. She is too short to reach the box," I dared to reply.

He raised the butt of the gun like he was about to strike me in the head with it when Miss, looking curiously down at the whole interaction, stopped him.

"Now, Carl...you are causing a scene, and we all have work to return to. Another time, okay?" she purred towards him.

He lowered the gun and went back to standing in his protective position. He pulled a face towards me, telling me I had lucked out today.

I could feel Miss staring at me as I carefully reached back into the box again. I wondered what she was calculating or if she was taking note of me for some future psychotic purpose.

"I'll let you off with a warning...this time, Raya—" she said in a hushed tone, while bending down towards me, but then raised her voice and her body back up, "—but the next time you help someone, you will receive a demerit."

She said it loud enough to deter anyone else from assisting another person. The fact that she knew my name made my chest instantly tighten in anxiety. She had only ever spoken to me once when she gave me my laundry assignment, so I couldn't quite comprehend why she would remember me, let alone know my name.

Even with the burden of this reflection, I had to keep going, and since I was closer to the end of the line, I could see a glimpse of the men from N block as we walked past the stage back into our section of the building. I didn't see anyone I recognized because my view was blocked beyond the last row of men standing there, shivering.

Even if he were alive, I wouldn't be able to find my dad in this obscure visibility. I could only pray that he had seen me and was satisfied knowing I was surviving.

I walked back into the dismal building and lined up behind Shiri, who had already wrapped her gray coat around her waist. I was too depressed to address her, and when she turned to speak to me, I knew she could sense defeat in the manner that I held the jacket to the floor, dragging it like it wasn't a precious commodity.

"Pick it up, Raya, or they will take it from you," she warned before turning back around.

Guide showed up and escorted us to the Laundry Center.

While we walked, I tied the coat around my waist, as Shiri had done, and double-knotted it. I knew she was right, but she wasn't talking about the guards...she was talking about the other sisters. They would take it from me if I displayed that I could care less about it. Then, I would freeze to death in the coming months, literally. I couldn't let a few moments of weakness dictate my duration through the upcoming frigid temperatures.

The day stretched on like it had done the day before and the day before that. Shiri and I talked very little, even during the dinner hour. I just wasn't in the mood to converse about anything. I felt stuck in an endless cycle of misery and had nothing to look forward to. No one was coming for us, and I was too laden with regrets to formulate any type of escape, especially knowing the consequences of failure.

I walked in the same circle out in the yard after we ate, then went to the same cell and lay in the same bunk to await the same routine tomorrow.

Rio wasn't there when I got to our cell, but within another hour or so, she showed up with her coat sleeves rolled up so far back it was almost comical. I didn't hear her trying to remove it, either.

Without a word, she went straight to bed.

She fell asleep fairly quickly, but I had no such bliss. I lay in my bunk listening to her breathing deeply, envious of her temporary peace, but then she started to whimper and cry loudly for her mom and dad. She sounded like she was experiencing a night terror, but I didn't want her to get in trouble for making too much noise...even if she couldn't help it. I hopped down and decided to shake her gently awake.

Once she began to recognize me and her surroundings, I asked her if she was okay.

"I wanna go home, Raya, but my mommy and daddy aren't dere. They went to heaven in the fire. Miss said heaven isn't wheal. Where did my mommy and daddy go den?" she innocently asked between sniffles.

"Did Miss tell you that today? Is that why you are so upset?" I questioned back.

She nodded slowly while looking deeply into my eyes. She was searching for a different answer from someone she could trust.

This was the first time Rio had ever mentioned her parents or any of her family, for that matter. I was too desensitized to process that this baby might as well be an orphan when I answered, "Hopefully, your mommy and daddy are awaiting judgment in Abraham's bosom[1] . Miss doesn't know the Most High as we know Him. She doesn't believe the truth of the Bible like we do."

"Why?" Rio asked.

Her eyes were full of inquisitive wonder.

I had to think hard to formulate an answer that would satisfy her and hopefully stop the questioning.

We both needed our rest.

"Everybody isn't taught the same thing, Rio," I answered. "But the Most High can open anyone's eyes that He chooses. He hasn't chosen her yet. Just pray for her."

"Okay," she snorted.

I zipped up her coat and wrapped the blankets around her like a burrito to get her comfortable and hopefully

---

1. Luke 16:22

back to sleep. Then, I told her the story of Joseph and how he endured while imprisoned[2].

Someone nearby shushed me harshly before, from a distance, I overheard the squeak of boots on the floor, no doubt from a guard. I abruptly stopped and looked down at Rio. She was thankfully fast asleep. I stealthily jumped back into my bunk and pretended to be snoring.

The noise of the guard went by quickly and forcefully, but I stayed in my rested position until I actually dozed off.

---

2. Genesis 40

SEVENTEEN

— ● —

SOLO

It could've easily been Raya lying there on her deathbed instead.

Juda's lying there on his deathbed instead.

Juda's dying instead.

The words tumbled around in my brain like a dryer on the fluff cycle.

I got down on my knees next to my bunk bed and prayed fervently all night.

I couldn't sleep.

I had no peace.

That girl's words eroded my soul, whittling me down to nothingness.

I didn't know if she was prophesying Juda's death or just talking out the side of her neck.

I asked the Father to show me what I was not seeing.

I asked Him for understanding and acceptance if Juda was being taken from the land of the living but, in the same breath, begged Him to save my cousin if He saw fit.

It had been two days since Maya destroyed what little harmony I had left in me.

I carefully got up from the floor and walked in place for a little while to straighten out the knots and alleviate the stiffness in my legs and knees.

It was late morning, well past breakfast time, so I didn't attempt to go to the kitchen for food. I didn't care about food.

Why should I eat?

I rambled up the stairs to my Lookout, where I had violently thrown my phablet after Lillian and Maya left the other day.

I didn't care about notifications or transcripts or security feeds.

I just wanted my family back.

I flopped down in front of the monitors, unsure why I even came up here.

Nothing was appealing.

Nothing in here mattered.

But at the same time, I wasn't ready to face Juda's comatose body today. I didn't know what to talk to him about or if I could find any words to say at all.

I mindlessly swirled in my chair, ignoring all the flashing red lights on the monitors. I had no idea where my phablet landed, but I wasn't ready to search for it.

Ms. Lynn poked her head into my room without knocking and presented a plate of rehydrated cube steak with gravy over rice.

I thanked her and set the plate on one of my workbenches, not even remotely interested, although it smelled mouthwateringly delicious.

"Have you got any news bout Raya?" she asked, noting my reaction to the plate.

She didn't hound me to eat, but when I saw her insulted facial expression, I decided that I would try to force it down later.

"No, ma'am. I guess she is having a hard time, just like the rest of us," I responded, not understanding what Ms. Lynn expected me to say.

"Baby, you ain't alone. You know that, right? We all know it's rough on you most of all. Matter fact, come here," she demanded.

I slowly picked myself up out of the chair and walked towards her, but I didn't feel like a hug was supportive enough.

I wanted a miracle, but unfortunately, she couldn't put that on a plate and offer it to me.

She didn't reach out for a hug but grabbed my hands and held them tightly while she spoke, "Now, I don't claim to be religious much, but one thing I do know is that Gawd can do all things, but He ain't no genie in a bottle. You don't get yo wishes granted right away. Be patient, and you will find out He does what's best for all of us in due time. You hear me?"

Her gaze was piercing through my depression. This woman had seen me and spoke directly to my low spirit.

"Yes, ma'am," I replied truthfully.

"Okay then," she concluded, letting go of my hands. "If you need anything, we're all here for you, and don't you ever doubt it, young man."

With that, she turned and left me with the plate and went towards the Infirmary to carry out her daily visitation with Juda.

I sat back down in my chair, in wonder at her words. They were like a soothing balm on cracked skin.

I needed to hear them.

I rolled the chair closer to review the monitors, but before I could focus on the blinking alarms, Big Man and Farmer John demanded my attention.

"Any updates on Raya?" Big Man questioned, a little too comfortable barging into my security room.

"I was just about to look," I started as I retrained my eyes back toward the screens.

Before I could check Raya's latest transcripts, I noticed a mission alert glaring at me. I opened it up and read that the Syndicate was planning an attack for today in under two hours. If I had my phablet with me yesterday, I would have caught it, and we would have had more time to plan.

I sighed deeply in response to my own immature reactions.

I explained to Big Man and John that a family reunion was being targeted this afternoon, and if a team left within the next ten minutes, they could make it to the park where the event was scheduled.

They looked at each other in quick deliberation and decided to risk it.

"How many people? Which park? How far is it?" John rattled off.

"I don't know. Greenwood State Park. It's 45 miles away, east of I-75. I can get you there, but like I said...y'all need to leave in ten minutes to make it before the soldiers," I responded while skimming over all the information before me.

"Let's go find Jose and James," Big Man said to John, then turned to me. "I need you to open the vault, Solo. We will need four handguns and a Bowie."

I got up immediately to get what he requested.

By the time I left the vault with the weapons, John, Big Man, James, and Jose were waiting impatiently in the tunnel. I gave them each a gun and gave the knife to Big Man.

I asked him for his birthday in exchange.

"Why is that important right now?" he asked, irritated for being held up.

"I need to set a code for you to get back in through the exit hatch," I answered, equally irritated for being questioned.

"It's today, November 3rd. I was born in 1992," he rapidly answered.

I went to the Lookout and gathered the four keys to the ATVs situated nearest the exit. After handing them over, the men started jogging towards the exit hatch with everything in tow.

"Wait!" I yelled after Big Man.

When he turned in my direction, he jogged backward. I threw him a two-way radio so we could stay in touch.

I pulled up the Sanctuary's security program and logged Big Man's birthday as an authorized user, then pulled up an aerial map to help navigate them to the correct park.

I went to transfer the data to my phablet so I could go sit with Juda and explain the mission to him, play-by-play. But my pocket was empty, and it didn't dawn on me immediately that the phablet was somewhere behind my workbench.

My pulse quickened, and my blood pressure rose slightly, thinking about the lost device.

Mentally, I retraced my steps until I recalled myself heaving the phablet across the room in frustration. I went to the workbench and started shoving it out of the way. Behind dusty cobwebs, I located it and gripped it in the safety of my hand. After swiping all the debris from it, I noticed a tiny hairline crack spidering across the screen.

Great...

After trying to turn it on, the red battery light flashed a few times, indicating it was dead.

I sighed loudly and put it on the charger.

Now, I would have to wait a bit before visiting Juda.

"Solo, I could use some directions, if you don't mind," Big Man's voice came through the radio.

I could hear the wind rushing past him as he rode full speed on his ATV.

"Got it. You need to head due east once you get near the interstate. Due. East. Don't deviate," I responded while marking out the map.

Big Man didn't respond, so I decided to clear the other alarms that were flashing.

The water filtration system showed that it was time to empty the pre-sediment strainer again, and there was a semi-loose water supply connector with the main valve alerting. I would have to repair that before the sun went down, marking the beginning of the Sabbath.

The ventilation system needed an authorization code to switch over to a forced air system for heat. I quickly plugged that in because the temperature down here was starting to signify winter had arrived. I set it to remain at a steady 72 degrees to ensure everyone would be comfortable.

Then I saw pages and pages of continuous transcripts from Raya transmitting in. I read the last few paragraphs, but decided to read the rest on my phablet when I could dedicate enough time to dissect the information coming in.

As I read, all the blood drained down to my toes.

I pulled out the headset from beside the secondary monitor and switched on the live audio feed.

Once I put on the headphones, I listened long enough to want to cut off my own ears. I threw the headset as far away from me as the cords would allow and switched it back to the silent transcripts.

Raya was being tortured.

I promptly stretched out on the floor and began praying against every wicked, demonic thing I heard through the audio feed. If there were something I could invent to cast its remembrance out of my brain, I would do it straightaway and without fail. I rebuked every abominable utterance I heard, not only for myself but for Raya.

As I pleaded my case to the Most High, I felt the edges of sleep caressing me like my mother did when I was a child. I had forced myself awake for more than forty-eight hours and couldn't hold out any longer.

My body had no choice but to fall into its warm enticement.

"Solo...boy, get up. Get up!"

Big Man was shaking my torso roughly with his boot.

I opened my eyes and noticed my left cheek squashed into the carpeting. I lifted my head slightly, brushed away the crust from the corner of my mouth, and felt the indented divots from the flooring on the side of my face.

I got up slowly, still overtired, stumbling to stand upright.

Big Man was wearing a disappointed scowl, but as soon as he saw me struggling to gain control of myself, his face softened.

"When was the last time you slept?" he asked in a more controlled tone.

"Three days ago," I replied, my voice broken and hoarse. "What happened? How did you get back so fast?"

He explained that they were gone for almost six hours and got lost along the way. I never responded on the two-way, but thankfully, John had been to Greenwood State Park once before and recognized some of the landmarks.

"It was too late when we got there. The Syndicate took who they were gonna take and left the rest for the burial truck. We barely made it out before it pulled up," he explained.

If he was trying to make me feel guilty, he was overachieving.

"I...I sincerely apologize. I don't know what happened. One minute, I was praying, and the next...it's all my fault.

Everything is all my fault," I agonized with a sudden deep frown creasing across my forehead.

Before I could storm out of the room, angry at my shortcomings, Big Man grabbed me by the shoulders.

"Hey! You didn't do it on purpose, son. I forgive you. Now forgive yourself. Don't carry all this negative weight around. You keep blaming yourself for everything when you don't know what the Most High has planned. Everything has a purpose and a place. Stay the course, Solo," he demanded.

He looked me in the eyes and wouldn't let go until I acknowledged his words.

I nodded at him weakly.

"I mean it," he said while loosening his grip on my shoulders.

I hung my head but tried my best to man up under pressure.

The fully charged phablet caught my attention, and I moved to unplug it.

The constant transcripts from Raya were pouring in, but these I deleted immediately.

I didn't have it in me to tell Big Man that Raya was actively being brainwashed with demonic chanting and recitations.

"It's about time for the Sabbath to begin. I'm gonna go see Juda," I said, excusing myself from the situation.

Big Man didn't try to stop me and moved out of the way as I passed.

It was a short walk, but I dragged my feet the whole way, making the trip longer than necessary.

After arriving, I saw no one else was there, and the lights were partially dimmed. I pulled the chair, which had been moved closer to the wall, back to the side of Juda's bed.

After situating myself in the hard plastic seat, I told Juda all about the failed mission, Raya's torture, and how inadequate I felt.

I sat there for a long time, not knowing what else to say when I noticed Juda's right hand was drooping off the side of the bed.

I took hold of it to place it back at his side, and as I centered his arm, he squeezed my hand.

I'm trippin'.

I placed my arm at a better angle like we were shaking hands, then right away, he squeezed my hand again.

I dropped his hand and ran for the door.

"ADINA! MIRA!"

Eighteen

Angel

A VA WATCHED ME CLOSELY from the doorway as I stuffed the last of my belongings into my worn overnight bag.

"I still think you need to stay a bit longer. We could really use the help, you know. There is still an issue with Derek learning all the security protocols. I think a few more days of training will get him on track," she threw at me.

I zipped up the bag, tossed it across my right shoulder, and then turned to face her.

"It's time for me to go, Ava. I've waited long enough. You and Jeremiah got this. You don't need me anymore. Derek will learn with practice...not preaching," I tirelessly explained.

She folded her arms defiantly as if she were getting ready to block my departure, but as I moved closer to where she stood, she relented and sidestepped out of my path.

I continued up the stairwell until I reached the main level. Ava was hard on my heels, still trying to convince me to stay, but I stopped listening long before we made it to the tunnel.

I walked towards the vault, stood before the keypad, and entered the code. The keypad lit green, and I could hear the locking mechanism unlatch.

Once inside, I retrieved a few boxes of ammo for my trusty .22. The glass encasement held my attention from the corner of my eye, and I turned to Ava, who was still following me.

"I just remembered something—" I said while handing her a slip of paper, "—this is the code for the vault. Don't share this with anyone. Only you and Jeremiah should have this code. If anything ever alarms, get the journal behind the glass there."

I pointed to the encasement.

"What is that?" Ava questioned bluntly.

"It's trust," I responded, not wanting to cause a panic, but at the same time, I couldn't possibly explain further.

After dealing with me for over a month, Ava had garnered enough discernment to know when to push me further and when to hold back.

She held her peace and just nodded.

"Can you at least tell me your plans? Should we ever expect to see you again?" Ava asked instead.

"Most High willing, we will meet again," was my only response.

After closing the vault, she walked down a portion of the tunnel next to me, but we ultimately stopped near the park. This signaled that our paths would split here.

I hugged her, not wanting her to think I was abandoning them without a reasonable cause.

Ava was like a true sister now.

She had nursed me back to health and supported every arrangement I suggested for the body as a whole. She didn't press me for information when it wasn't warranted, and I really appreciated and enjoyed her company.

Under normal circumstances, I felt that we would have been the best of friends.

"You know, when you first showed up at my house, I thought Jay was trying to move in another wife without my consent," Ava divulged, unprompted.

I gave her a shocked look and then burst out laughing.

"So that's why you were so hesitant around me at first?" I speculated, still laughing slightly.

She nodded and returned an amused smile.

"I'm glad that wasn't the case, but I have grown to love you as a close friend and sister. I'm grateful that the Most High placed you on our path," Ava concluded.

She reached for my hand and squeezed it.

I hoped that our sisterhood would remain unscathed if we were to ever meet again.

Without any further delay, I turned to walk down the lonely exit tunnel, anxious to get back to the brightness of sunshine and coolness of wind on my skin that being above ground afforded.

I didn't look back, but I knew Ava had the same stinging tears in her eyes that I did.

Nineteen

---•---

Raya

I opened my heavy eyelids to the constant hammering on the cell bars as the night guard walked through. The fluorescent lights automatically turned on, persecuting my eyes. I tried to shield them with my deeply scorched hands.

As soon as I inhaled my first conscious breath, my sensory awareness was invaded by the odor of urine.

Rio had peed on herself.

She had involuntarily chosen the worst moment to have an accident, and we had no time to counter the inevitable consequences of it.

I glanced over at the one banging her baton and shouting for us to 'rise and grind.' I was not very familiar with this guard. She worked the night shift sparingly and wasn't usually the one to commence the morning wake-up call. That task was typically reserved for Dark Shades, but she was nowhere to be seen.

Maybe it was her day off.

I had hoped Dark Shades would appear and somehow protect Rio like she had done weeks ago.

Maybe even show her a little leniency.

When Rio roused herself from bed and realized her mistake, she reacted in a screaming meltdown, trying to irrationally remove the clothes from her tiny body as quickly as she could. She was terrified of what would happen to her in the Chute.

Even though she was only four years old, she knew sometimes people would not return.

I jumped down from our shared bunk and tried to console and shush her tantrum. I fought to keep her from ripping off her clothes. While attempting to reason with her, I firmly pulled her hands down to her sides to neutralize her, but her animalistic fear was so intense that she began scratching my arms distrustfully in resistance.

Her episode attracted the attention of the night guard immediately, and she radioed her counterparts to delay the cells' automatic opening and for them to send backup. She removed a key from her hip pocket and quickly unlocked our singular cell.

When she noticed Rio's dank-smelling uniform, she pulled out her demerit device and plugged in Rio's prisoner number.

"Oh, dearie, that's a day in the Chute for you," the cynical-looking brunette woman declared in a contradictorily babyish way.

She was completely unsympathetic to Rio's age and lack of control over her bodily functions. Looking down at her with a hard-hearted glare, she moved to jerk Rio's arm from my hold.

Rio physically reacted by amping up her tantrum. She began to seize and recoil from all human contact. I had to let her go because I couldn't maintain a grip on her any longer. She retreated to the far corner of the tiny room in a haze of wild thrashings.

The guard then had to fully enter our cell to reclaim her.

Ignoring me, she extended her truncheon, ready to beat the child into submission before taking her away to the torturous Chute.

When I saw her intentions with the baton, my insides hardened to stone, and my brain's synapses all fired at once.

Memories of my brother succumbing to his death flashed across my mind's eye.

When I lost Juda, I lost all will to fight, but that drive to protect the innocent rushed back to me like a rage of pure energy, provoked by the guard raising her arm to administer the first blow.

In that split second, before she hit Rio, I mustered all my strength and dealt her a roundhouse kick to the head from behind, complete with a guttural outcry arising from deep within.

The sheer force of the unexpected hit caused her to stagger towards the toilet, tripping herself.

I didn't allow her the chance to regain her balance when I jumped on top of her, knocking her to the ground. With a loud thud, her head struck the unsanitary toilet on the way down, and I repeatedly dealt her concussive blows to the face.

"DON'T TOUCH HER! DON'T YOU EVER TOUCH HER! I'LL KILL YOU!" I heard myself roaring while abandoning all sense of sanity.

I could see my brother dying, over and over, in my memories, and I firmly felt I had somehow traded Juda for Rio at that moment.

I was doing to the guard what I should have done to the soldier before he murdered my brother.

I felt the snapping of tiny facial bones against my fists as I wailed on her. Her bloodied face was becoming unrecognizable when I felt the first attack from behind.

A hard object struck me in the back several times before I realized someone else had joined the fray.

There were some faint cheers for recompense coming from the other cells, but I ignored all.

I transferred my anger towards the first guard, redirecting it towards the second. As I shielded myself from the blows of the billy club, I noticed that it was Karen bestowing them. Her expression was of disturbing pleasure as she relished in the targeted strikes.

My adrenaline didn't allow me to fully appreciate the pain dealt from her weapon yet, so I bellowed out another war cry and lunged at her with full force. She was unsuspecting of this reaction and faltered in her attack.

As she hesitated, I was given the advantage of forcing her to the ground onto her back. Her baton, knocked from her hands, rolled across the gray floor away from us. I punched her in the side of the head while she tried to guard her face with her hands.

She cowardly pleaded for mercy.

The same mercy she was never willing to give.

I was getting ready to repeat my assault tactics against Karen when I took another hit from behind, but this subtle attack astonished me greatly.

Electric voltage seared through my nervous system, causing my whole body to spasm in throbbing agony.

I had to grit my teeth to retain consciousness.

There was no way I would allow myself to pass out. I had committed to protecting Rio at all costs and was now paying the full price, but I still had the driving need to affirm the child would be okay, even after all of this.

Karen used her knees to remove me from her, and I fell to my side, still under the electrical ambush. I could only brace myself against it, using sheer willpower.

When she regained her footing, Karen kicked me in the stomach in retaliation.

My eyes watered from the immense struggle to stay awake, and a thin line of drool escaped my lips in exertion.

Miss was standing over me, forever observing. She held the trigger end of the taser, allowing the barbs to continue their purpose.

When she eventually released the charge, I breathed greedily as if I had been held underwater and was finally allowed air.

She looked irate at Karen and commanded that she clean up the 'mess' in my cell while she escorted me to the Chute because, apparently, she had to do everything around here herself.

Karen wiped her mouth, nodded begrudgingly, and then pulled me to my feet. My balance was wavering, but I resolved not to let them see me break down, so I willed my legs to remain upright.

"I'm very disappointed in you, Raya."

Miss clicked her tongue to relay it.

"I had such high hopes for you, but I suppose you are your father's child, after all. Come along...we have much to do today," she sang out to me spitefully.

"Rio..." I managed to breathe out, confused by her resentful words about my father.

One thing at a time, Raya.

I could still hear the fragile cries of the scared little girl coming from the far corner of our cell.

"Oh, don't worry about that little pest. You will take her place in the Chute, but I'm afraid you must undertake two days instead of one. I know, I know...this is your first infraction, but alas, you almost killed poor Rebecca. I can't let that go for a mere one or two demerits, now can I?" she delusionally reasoned.

Miss walked towards the inner hallway and looked back at me for compliance, but my feet were firmly planted.

I was still perplexed by her sing-songy way of relaying insults and information.

"If you wish to resist, I can always bring the tiny piss ant to the Chute alongside you. You clearly have a soft spot for her. I can place you right next to one another if you want to listen to her pathetic screams for two days. Your choice," Miss stated and turned to continue her journey to the heart of the Program's structure.

I no longer hesitated to follow her to my fate.

She smiled proudly to herself and clasped her hands behind her back, signifying I was no longer a valid threat, and she needed no further precautions.

We continued walking down the gray hallway steadily, but in due time, Miss had to slow for me because my walk was shifting to a heavy shuffle. The adrenaline was wearing off, and I could feel every ache in my sinew and bones. My body had become brittle from the effects of starvation, dehydration, and being overworked.

"Don't worry. You will be able to sit soon," she offered with mischief underlining her words.

I didn't have it in me to respond.

Whatever lay ahead for me, I reasoned, was well worth it to protect Rio.

We stopped once we arrived in front of a compact elevator. Miss pressed the 'up' button, but there was no wait before the doors opened and we ushered in.

For a glimmer of a second, while she pressed the top floor button, I thought perhaps I could take her down. But as I attempted to raise my arms towards her thick neck, I felt the weakness draining me and quickly abandoned the notion.

We jerked upwards slightly, with her humming to herself and examining her nailbed while we waited to exit.

As the door chimed our arrival and opened to the level housing the Chute, my nose was instantly assaulted with the stench of rotting flesh and human excrement.

I could hear shrieking screams from enclosures several feet ahead of us.

There was a windy feeling to the room, causing me to shiver. I was grateful that I had slept in my recently issued coat.

Miss unnecessarily pushed me out of the elevator towards a long walkway that connected to the enclosures.

As we navigated the walkway, I saw a scrawny-looking man hunched over, bleeding from his lip. He was about to be placed inside an enclosure by two male guards when he began yelling nonsense about an angel and passports he had made for her. He cried out for freedom in exchange for valuable information.

"Nice try, Antoine, but that's not how this works," one of them maniacally replied before pushing him into the tiny box and locking it behind him with a heavy padlock.

I could still hear him calling out for mercy, but his pleas landed on unfeeling, deaf ears.

The other guard pushed a black button atop the enclosure, amplifying Antoine's screams.

The guards walked away laughing.

As they passed us to get back to the single elevator, they both averted their eyes in acknowledgment of Miss.

Apparently, everyone was either terrified or in complete awe of this formidable woman lunatic.

Miss pointed to the far right cage, indicating that I place myself inside.

I nervously complied and walked towards it, realizing just how claustrophobic my new confinement would be.

I entered the dark hole of a box and sat down on the only bench in there. The room was set up like an actual dunking booth, with the bench suspended in the air. Just like Dani had described.

I looked down and couldn't see an ending, only a chute-like shaft. My legs were dangling under the metal bench. The walls were blank, except for a mid-sized red button to my right that read 'Release'.

Around the button were names scratched into the drywall.

So many names.

It didn't take a rocket scientist to figure out what happened when the release button was pressed.

As Miss moved to shut the enclosure door, closing me into utter darkness, one name caught my attention.

"*Dani...*" I whispered under my breath.

I grappled with a sinking realization.

She had released herself.

"I hope you take the time to reflect on what you've done, Raya. I believe we can break you, yet," she mockingly pledged, shutting and locking the door like she had just placed a turkey in the oven. She audibly pressed the button on top of my cage to begin my cook time.

As she walked away, I could hear her booted heels clopping against the floor but not back toward the elevator. She had made her way to Antoine's box, pushing the button to make his screaming cease.

It seemed as if she would be granting him freedom after all.

Meanwhile, I couldn't appreciate why Dani would resort to such a thing, but soon, I had another horrible realization as demonic chantings and incantations began playing loudly in my booth to a rhythmic tempo.

The chantings were repetitive and got louder and louder. I couldn't make out my own thoughts, and something was spiritually blocking me from praying. My brain turned to melted wax every time I tried calling out to the Most High for help.

It was pitch black, but after a few minutes of the demonic chants, pictures began flashing around the walls of talismans and demented, contorted people.

There were no breaks in between the noise and pictures.

Even though I closed my eyes as tight as I could, the images were in a specific brightness that penetrated my eyelids. There was no escape from the torture except the looming release button.

I was ultimately given a choice to endure forty-eight hours of this or send myself to the gates of Hades.

After struggling to pray for hours, I screamed in maddening torment. Louder and louder until I lost my voice, all in hopes of drowning out the sounds.

TWENTY

—◦—

ANGEL

"I JUST DON'T UNDERSTAND why you need all these forks, Peaches. We have forks," I laughingly commented to my favorite cousin.

She was packing bags to take to Georgia, and I thought she would need a freight container, the way she prioritized her possessions.

"Well, just in case," she said while shrugging her stout shoulders and placing the forks into Ziplock bags.

"Can you please get her off this 'Lot's wife'[1] ledge, Marcus?" I asked her husband, who was sitting on a couch, watching our exchange in amusement.

"You the one who came here upheaving everything. That's your problem, right there," he said through his playful smile. "I got my ONE bag packed."

---

1. Gen 19:25,26

He had his arms laid across the top of the sofa and his legs stretched out in front of him while he switched between the news and his wife's shenanigans.

"Peaches, if we're gonna make it to Georgia by nightfall, we need to leave in less than an hour. Can you please just take what you absolutely need? You know...like clothes, pictures, and money?" I urged.

She looked over at me, putting her hands on her hips.

I could visibly see the sweat glistening off her forehead and across the bridge of her nose. After deliberating, she swiped at both with her bare hands, removing some moisture.

"I just don't know, Angel. I've never had much, and now you want me to drop everything and run, basically. I need a second," she responded while deserting the forks.

I watched my cousin pace the kitchen.

Her butter pecan brown skin was more sun-kissed than usual, compliments of the hours spent outside tending the container garden she was trying to maintain on her concrete patio.

She finally walked towards her bedroom, commenting that she would be ready in thirty minutes.

I knew that meant an hour.

I smiled warmly at her demeanor as she left the room. She was much the same as I remembered if not a little plumper and a bit more easygoing.

If this were before she met Marcus, I probably would have had to knock her out and stuff her into the car to make her leave everything behind.

After I explained how the Syndicate was, and still is, kidnapping mass groups of believers, Marcus all but hopped into my truck to head out.

It took a little bit more convincing to get Peaches on board.

I was still standing in the kitchen when Marcus called out to me from the open-concept living room, "By the way, why do y'all call her Peaches? She still won't tell me. I've been trying to get that story out of her for years."

That memory was in the far recesses of my brain, but it was still relevant to my cousin's personality now.

"If I tell you, she might kill me. But then again, if you know, you will understand her a little better," I replied.

I moved over to a faded green recliner in the living room. It was, no doubt, something she had saved from a thrift store, and he allowed it in order to appease her habits.

"We were extra poor growing up. She and her mom more than the rest of my dad's side of the family. Even as a child, she was always bigger than the rest of us, and we could never figure out how. They barely had food at home and mostly ate from food pantries when they did get to eat. Peaches' house would always smell like overripe fruit when we came over to play, but no one could ever find the source of that smell until one day, her mom opened up a loose panel in her closet when she was cleaning out Peaches' room. She was stealing peaches from the orchard across the street and saving them to eat when she was alone and hungry. Her mom made her go tell the owner what she was doing, and she ended up having to pick peaches for him for a month to work off what she had stolen," I explained.

"That wasn't so bad. I thought you were gonna tell me something crazy. I kinda figured her...collecting...was deep-rooted to something along those lines. We're working on it, though. Most High willing, she will get better with time," Marcus responded.

"Well, the time has come. Where we're going, she won't be able to collect much of anything else," I quipped.

A lull developed in our conversation, so we both naturally went back to watching the news, captivated by the latest developments.

Several channels were featuring watchdog snapshots of the riots happening all over the country. They were spotlighting the vast amount of missing ethnic workers. From the tone of the reports, the remaining citizens didn't seem to care much about the actual missing people but rather how it affected the economy.

Small businesses and mid-size corporations were losing human capital as well as their majority supply of consumers. More giant corporations and private investors within them were gaining profits by leaps and bounds, widening the gap between the rich and the poor.

Former so-called middle-class citizens were finding themselves struggling to eat, and they didn't understand why. The masses were demanding answers from the government while the government remained historically silent.

Peaches emerged from the back of the house an hour later with an overstuffed duffle bag. She was grappling with it through the audible gritting of her teeth, grunts, and groans. She barely had a handle on it. When her struggle finally registered in Marcus' ears, he popped up from the couch and met her halfway, taking the bag out of her hands.

"Whatcha got in here, woman? Bricks?" he questioned while setting the duffle bag by the front door.

She crumpled her face into a sour expression at his comment.

He was unsuccessfully trying to lighten the mood while she was visibly on the verge of an anxiety attack over leaving so much stuff behind.

Not knowing what else to do to alleviate her trepidation, he nervously eyed the door as an escape before taking their bags out to the bed of my truck.

After loading everything of immediate worth to Peaches, we piled into the truck's cab, with her occupying the middle of the faded bench seat. She had a bag full of fruit, water, and other snacks cradled in her lap, so we didn't have to stop before we reached the state line between Alabama and Georgia.

"You sure you don't wanna drive, Marcus? I have counterfeit passports for both of y'all, in case we get pulled over. It should be fine if you wanna drive. I got stopped on the way to Texas last month, but my papers checked out. They are pretty decent fakes," I looked over to the passenger side and implored him.

"You got it. I'm gonna take a nap. Wake me up when we get past Mississippi. I'll drive the second leg from there," he answered.

I nodded and put the gear in drive.

True to his word, Marcus was fast asleep shortly after we pulled off. His head was suspended and drooping in front of him like an old man who fell asleep reading the newspaper.

No matter.

Me and my favorite cousin spent those hours bliss-fully catching up on each other's lives and laughing at our memories from childhood.

The windows were slightly rolled down, and the cool November air pleasantly slapped us across the face.

It felt like freedom in the wind.

With Peaches to keep me company, I forgot our im-minent danger, being on the open road like this for a long while.

That was until I saw the flashing blue and red lights of an all-black, unmarked police cruiser.

My heart cinched momentarily, and I slowed to a stop on the shoulder of the interstate.

"We weren't speeding, were we?" Peaches questioned in an almost-whisper, confused as to why we were being randomly stopped.

"No, we weren't. I told you already. If you're darker than them, that's an automatic red flag. That's why I prefer driving at night," I hissed back.

I looked over at Marcus, who was roused from his long doze by the sudden halt of the truck's movement.

Earlier, we had a heated debate about the best time to make the journey. I insisted on driving at night for this apparent reason, while he demanded daylight because he couldn't see that well traveling in unfamiliar places at night. I eventually relented to his needs, in opposition to my first mind.

I sighed in irritation that I had been proven right.

As the officer approached the truck, another un-marked cruiser arrived and pulled in front of us, then another to the side of us.

We were boxed in.

I looked down at the door and noticed my weapon was not placed in its usual home, and my nerves were instantly set on edge.

I thought quickly back to where I may have placed it, and I eventually recalled putting it on the bathroom counter at Peaches' house when I went to relieve myself before we left. I must have left it there absentmindedly.

I couldn't believe I had been so careless.

My heart began thumping wildly, doubling in speed, thinking of other ways I could try getting us out of this mess.

Something far beyond unexpected was transpiring.

I could feel it.

"Act natural," I demanded of my cousin and her husband as a figure approached the driver's side of the truck.

I saw the officer's looming shadow block out a portion of the sun from my left peripheral, but I continued to stare straight ahead.

He removed his shades and, in an unnervingly deep voice, asked for my passport and registration.

I turned to face him against the sunlight shining around him while gripping the beat up steering wheel.

"Well, well, well..." the officer said as I finally decided to look up towards him to smile, simper, and give him my best impression of innocence.

My veins turned to ice, my smile instantly evaporated, and I began to tremble in visible fear as recognition held me in its sudden grip.

He casually bent down, folding his suited arms across my window seal, and peered inside at me specifically.

"If it isn't the elusive Nora Hayes..." he trailed off, looking over at an approaching minion.

Another suited character had exited one of the black vehicles during the brief stare-off with me and was walking in our direction.

"Is it her, sir?" the shorter man asked.

He looked like a catalog model who didn't make the cut because of his height. He was a younger, handsome man who wore his all-black suit well, but he also had a strange marking tattooed on his neck that seemed out of place. It looked like a sophisticated gang symbol, almost resembling a recycling ideogram.

"It is indeed, Phillips. Agatha's information checked out, after all," he cheerfully answered.

Phillips motioned his hand with just two fingers wagging in the air. Suddenly, my truck was surrounded by suits with guns.

We had no choice but to get out and surrender with our hands high in the air.

"I've been looking for you for a long time, Mrs. Hayes. You're quite a busy woman, but I'm glad we finally meet again," the Commander of the Syndicate offered with a devious smirk.

What he recalled as 'meet' consisted of him permitting his soldiers to shoot and drag away the vast majority of my congregation, including my husband, the leader of our church, at the end of our Sabbath service back in July.

The memory of crouching over my lifeless husband while screaming in agony came to mind. My sheltered world came crashing down in just mere seconds because of the Commander.

I remembered him plucking me up aggressively from the ground by my hair and then hearing my daughter calling out to me in terror from a distance. I couldn't find her in the chaos of everything as he dragged me away towards his truck.

As I fought in vain for him to release his grip on me, I lost a few locs in the struggle.

My only consolation was the thought that my children could make it to the safety of the Sanctuary my husband had built for them if my son, Juda, followed all the protocols correctly.

I had barely escaped myself a few days later.

Even still, the Holy Spirit had guided me to activate all the sanctuaries Ezekiel had put into play instead of immediately returning to my children like I desperately wanted to.

It was the most challenging spiritual act of obedience ever required of me.

As we were handcuffed and shoved into separate cars, I wondered if I had done something to derail that obedience and was being punished for it, dragging my cousin and her husband down with me.

"I love you, Yasmine. Everything will be okay," Marcus called out to his wife before she disappeared through a tinted door.

I was pushed towards the Commander's vehicle, where he was waiting in the back to converse with me.

After the convoy pulled back onto the interstate, he began.

"I'll have to mark this day—November 3rd. The day I caught an angel," he laughingly said as we sped off to God-knows-where.

TWENTY-ONE

SOLO

I CHECKED RAYA'S TRANSCRIPTS for the fourth time this morning as I headed to the training room for 8 AM drills.

Finally, the data slowed to an average constant, with only a few sentences coming through simultaneously.

I praised the Father under my breath that my cousin's torture had finally ended because, for the past two days, the transcripts were nonstop.

I felt helpless and could only pray on her behalf.

I hoped she had the fortitude to fight against the brainwashing techniques.

I hoped she was praying as well.

I stepped into the training room, placed the phablet back in my pocket, and turned my attention to Farmer John.

I stood next to James, anticipating that he would partner with me on our regular stretch routine, but John loudly declared that we would do things differently today.

"TRUST is the very essence of our foundation. If you can't trust your team or yourself...well...what's the point of any jumping jack or sparring match? So, until we can gain each other's full trust, we won't be doing any more drills," he announced while slowly pacing back and forth.

There were some inaudible murmurings from a few people.

"Is that a problem?!" John shouted.

No one spoke up.

"Good...let's begin. Partner up with someone you don't know that well. Hurry up!"

I stood there, socially awkward, looking around for a partner.

Anyone in this room would do besides James. I didn't know anyone that well, compliments of a life mostly spent in the security room.

A young woman with her hair tied back in a puff walked up to me in a last-ditch effort to secure a partner.

"I guess we are the last two—partners?" she asked guardedly.

I nodded and introduced myself.

"Oh, I've heard of you—" she started, and my pride began to swell at being recognized, "You control the thermostat down here, right? Do you think you can turn up the heat a little bit more? I'm constantly freezing. My name is Sheba, by the way. Nice to meet you, Akhi.[1]"

That swell in my chest deflated at once. I guessed most people mistook me for the janitor down here.

"I'll see what I can do," was all I managed to respond.

I didn't feel we were getting off to a very trusty start.

I heard James snickering at our conversation from nearby. He had partnered with the older man, Charles.

We all quieted down when John began explaining our new mission.

"Every day, a set of you will run reconnaissance up top. We will map out a safe zone and a time grid of the best times to scout. You will be tasked with bringing a specific item back. Spend as much time getting to know your partner as possible. Understanding one another may be the key to your survival...since one of you will be blindfolded on the mission," he spelled out.

I stopped listening at that point.

I'm not doing this.

---

1. Hebraic word-my brother

"I'm looking forward to doing this!" Sheba squealed eagerly. "Aren't you?"

I feigned a polite smile at her without directly answering her question.

After John dismissed us, I said my goodbyes, then walked out of the training room towards the Infirmary to visit with Juda. Even though he had squeezed my hand days ago, he wasn't showing any other signs of improvement.

Mira said his hand squeeze could have been an involuntary muscle spasm, or it could have been the Most High working a miracle in him.

Only time would tell.

I was determined to faithfully wait for Juda to wake up. Afterward, we could take his recovery one step at a time. Meanwhile, I was getting close to masterminding an escape plan for Raya. After seeing what the Syndicate had done to her and probably had done to countless others, my sense of urgency ramped up threefold.

I pulled out my phablet and was about to type in my passcode when I felt I was being followed and watched.

Sheba was at my side, peering over my arm down at the device.

"What's that?" she asked.

I gave her an incredulous facial response.

"What? Didn't you hear what Sergeant John said? We need to get to know each other for our mission. We don't know when our turn will be, so I suggest we get this over with quickly," she babbled out.

I didn't realize my legs had autopiloted me to the Infirmary and stopped at the entry.

"I...can't right now. I don't think I'm gonna be a good partner for you. Maybe you should team up with another group," I decided out loud.

"I see. I'm not good enough for the maintenance man. Figures..." she sarcastically muttered, folding her arms deliberately and looking squarely at the ground.

"It's not that—" I sighed, "Let's start over. My name is Solo. I'm not the maintenance man, doorkeeper, janitor, or whatever else you think I am. Yes, I control the temperature, but that's only because I built the system. In fact, I built all the systems. My uncle created this place, and my cousin, right there, is fighting for his life while my other cousin...his sister...was snatched from us by the Syndicate when she put her life on the line for a would-be defector. I'm trying my best to bust her out of their detention center. So, if you will excuse me, I'm just a wee bit too busy to worry about this so-called 'trust' exercise."

My tone had increased from calm to crazed with every sentence of my continued rant until I sounded like I was yelling at her in frustration.

She looked at me like a deer in headlights, suspended by unease, before silently storming off.

I sighed again.

Great job, Solo. Can you do anything right?

"Wait!" I called out after her, but she didn't stop marching down the stairwell until she got to the community room. Then, she abruptly turned to face me again.

"You know, you aren't the only person with stuff going on. I lost my entire family in an instant just a few weeks ago. We were headed to the grocery store when a passport control blockade stopped us. Those Syndicate soldiers didn't care that we had the approved chipped passports. One of them recognized my dad as his prior supervisor. He clearly had an issue with a black man being in charge. Then he singled me out, asking me to choose...my family or my God. They left me in the car with the bodies. I don't know where I would be without the Holy Spirit guiding me to that tree. I'm just trying to do my part! I just want a purpose...a reason to go on!" Sheba all but screamed.

I felt three inches tall.

People were staring at us in curiosity.

"I know, and I'm sorry. Look, maybe we can create a schedule or something. I should be free in another hour if you still wanna consider partnering with me. Meet me in the training room?" I sheepishly appealed, trying to change the uncomfortable subject.

She stood there searching my face for sincerity.

Sheba then nodded ever so slightly before walking away towards the kitchen.

I grated my hands down my face in exasperation. I walked back up to the Infirmary, questioning how I could learn to trust someone I wasn't willing to understand.

I decided to give John's mission a try.

What can it hurt?

After sitting with Juda and narrating Raya's release and the misunderstanding with Sheba, I left.

I had hoped for some other sign of life today, but I was starting to get comfortable with this new reality. Everything would happen in the Most High's time...not mine.

I yielded myself to that certainty.

I inched my way toward the training room, taking my time to get there. I was still deep in thought about Raya when Sheba fell into step next to me.

"Penny for your thoughts?" she lightheartedly proposed.

"What?" I uttered, not aware of that outdated idiom.

She shook her head in response.

"Nevermind. My dad used to ask me that when he was wondering what was happening in my head."

"Did he always give you a penny, though? Seems a bit cheap," I jested in return.

She chuckled at my attempt to brighten the mood.

"So, what are you thinking exactly? Seems I interrupted your concentration...again," she questioned, trying her best to encourage me to share.

I had just elaborated everything to Juda and really didn't want to repeat myself to this girl I barely knew. Too much information was definite power if it got into the wrong hands. I wanted to learn how to trust her, but I wasn't about to start off blindly.

"Earlier, I told you the Syndicate took my cousin. I'm trying to build a digital blueprint of the facility where she is now. I have bits and pieces already, but it's not enough. I can hear her, but not much conversation happens in her daily routine. I can't quite put the puzzle pieces together," I explained carefully.

"How can you hear her?" Sheba ventured.

I explained the mole comms I invented and how the receiver was busted but not the transmitter.

"Can you show me? Is that okay?" she wondered.

I didn't feel any alarms going off in my spirit, so I agreed, persuaded that showing her the Lookout couldn't hurt anything. She probably wouldn't comprehend half the things she saw anyway.

We detoured to the Lookout, and I unlocked the door, allowing her entry.

She looked around, unfazed by the sheer number of gadgets, monitors, contraptions, and security feeds.

"So, this is what you do all day?" she baited with her nose slightly scrunched up.

She didn't seem too impressed by my brilliance.

A shiver of deficiency ran through my body and mind, but it was quickly replaced by open offense.

"Like you could do much better..." I scoffed under my breath.

She heard me and turned to justify her words.

"I didn't mean it like that—" she started, but I didn't let her finish.

"For your information, I can hack into just about any system; I've invented every luxury you have down here and more!" I interrupted, beyond annoyed at her passive-aggressive belittling.

As soon as I blurted all that out, I instantly regretted it.

Sheba shouldn't know those things about me.

She profoundly stared at me before taunting, "If you can hack into any system, why haven't you hacked into the security footage at your cousin's facility yet? Wouldn't that give you everything you need to know? But whatever. Genius."

My jaw dropped, then snapped shut in quiet amazement. My eyebrows raised to my hairline in pure wonder at the simplicity of her words.

Here I was, consumed in the complex notion that I had to rework the universe to secure Raya's release when it was all so painfully simple.

A smile of comical proportions crept across my face.

"Sheba...you're a genius!" I praised excitedly.

She shrugged her shoulders and fidgeted uncomfortably with being complimented for saying something meaningful.

"Yeah. No problem, I guess," she assented awkwardly.

"Uh. So, I actually need my privacy to do that, so—" I drawled out while nervously tapping my two pointer fingers together.

She seemed to comprehend that I was asking her to leave, but she didn't precisely budge either.

"I'm not going anywhere. You heard what John said. Besides, while you do whatever it is that you do, I can refresh your braids. I do hair, by the way, and whoever did yours last...well...bless their heart," she insisted, not realizing that I was the heart she was blessing.

I didn't have the overly assertive nature like Juda and couldn't find the right words to make her leave, so I relented and pulled up a chair for her to sit behind me.

She removed her backpack and started taking out combs and hair products, laying everything out on the closest workbench.

Initially, my nerves were on ten, and I began sweating under pressure, having someone so close while I worked. I never allowed it from anyone before, but soon after she started loosening my braids with a very tender hand, I relaxed and got straight to work, forgetting Sheba was even there.

She didn't press me to talk while we both completed our own masterpieces.

As she finished the last braid, I clapped my hands together once, turned around to face her, and exclaimed, "I'm in!"

Twenty-Two

Raya

8 AM. Sunday.

I stood in the shower stall, letting the water rain down my bruised body. I didn't bother with bathing.

There was no point.

There was no point to anything.

I could hear the hushed whispers of the other inmates looking over in my direction. Whispers about the girl who had no demerits but ended up in the Chute for two days for the attempted murder of a guard.

The hope of resistance seemed to have struck like a match in a dry forest. Everyone was in awe that a mere sixteen-year-old fought back so vehemently on someone else's behalf.

Even the guards were set on edge by hints and preparations of a potential riot.

No one said it, but I knew Guide was commanded to monitor my every move. So far, she had not left my side, not even now.

She was the one who freed me from the torture chamber and walked me cautiously to the washroom. Her body language never showed that she was afraid of me, but she was armed with an AR-15 when, previously, she only had the truncheon and demerit device.

When Dark Shades yelled out that wash day was over, I slowly exited the shower and wrapped the stiff gray towel around myself, never breaking eye contact with the mildewed floor. The tiles were almost black from the indelible mold, a welcome contrast to everything else's gray bleakness.

I wasn't aware if anyone was still paying attention to my movements, only focusing on the mundane task of drying off and getting dressed while stuck in my own depressive thoughts.

I could still hear the demonic words playing in my head long after they had stopped, and I still couldn't find the words to pray.

I thought my faith had always been unshakable, but I could understand Ryan's words describing his brainwashing as if his mind had been stretched out like chewing gum.

I was afraid even to question why God would allow me to endure it, but that question was bubbling dangerously close to the top of my meditations.

Guide handed me a uniform, and I studied my new prisoner number.

M115.

I knew Miss would never allow me to be anywhere near Rio again if she could help it, so I wondered why she let me stay in M block where I could, at least, keep an eye on the child from afar.

If Miss had done this strategically, she must have had plans to control me through the little girl.

A sick feeling punched me in the gut.

Miss would use and manipulate Rio to make me do whatever she bid. I had unwittingly consigned the child over to more incredible tortures than me.

If I had any tears left, I would shed them for what was inevitably in store for Rio, but I was too dehydrated, too parched to squeeze anything out.

Guide walked me to the Laundry Center, where I started robotically pushing soiled clothes into the washing machines. She stood there briefly, hoovering, but eventually decided to wait outside the door since cameras would pick up any disturbance I made.

Shiri moved towards my left side and also fed uniforms steadily into the industrial-sized washing machines.

As she bent down to pick up the next pile, she uttered, "Are you alright?"

It had been too long since I heard a friendly voice addressing me.

It was almost a foreign concept to reply.

I wasn't sure what she expected me to say since it was such a loaded question. Of course, I wasn't alright.

"Yeah."

I croaked the word out hoarsely, trying to clear my throat. My voice had not fully recovered from the hours' worth of screaming.

"Liar," she reprimanded, not caring that the cameras were watching.

"I'll be fine. I'm just tired, okay?" I affirmed, equally unbothered by the cameras.

The door to the Laundry Center opened, and I prepared myself to receive the demerit I knew was coming, but instead, Dark Shades entered and demanded a volunteer for construction detail.

When no one immediately stepped forward, she pointed me out and decreed, "You. The baldheaded one. Come with me."

I stuffed my last uniform into the machine and walked toward her in unquestioning compliance.

As we marched towards the men's section of the Program, my body was moving on autopilot through the hallway, wedged somewhat between Dark Shades and Guide. The strength I had just a week ago was evaporated entirely, along with all hope of enduring this place much longer.

I commiserated with Dani and her decision to release herself. Her dread of the Chute paralleled my recent experience, and I wasn't sure if I would make it out if there were to be a next time.

Dark Shades led us through a labyrinth of gray hallways until we reached a door to the rear of the Program's building. From what I could see, a few young men were mixing cement and repairing an alcove in the inner protective wall. The wall seemed to be crumbling from some sort of attack or strike.

As we neared, Dark Shades called out to the boys to focus on the repair, that I was there to stir the cement. Without hesitation, all four of them removed from the wheelbarrow and began parging the wall with the wet muck, working it back and forth with dull trowels.

"Use this shovel and move the cement around periodically so it doesn't dry up and get hard. You can handle that, can't you, Renegade?" Dark Shades taunted.

I picked up the shovel and did as she asked to demonstrate that I wasn't ignorant.

"Good. Keep at it," she concluded, leaving me under the watchful eye of Guide and returning inside the building.

I would stir the wet cement every few minutes and then watch the males work.

They all looked just as emaciated as the females, and I could relate to the slow dawdling of their work, knowing they had little to no real strength left either.

My arms felt like paver stones had burrowed under my skin, my movements stiff and weighted. I didn't want to be out here in the damp chilliness of November for eight hours, but I was grateful for the coat that had become like a second skin.

The young men came to collect the tacky cement periodically, but one kept lingering at the wheelbarrow. His eyes were constantly meeting mine, but he was hesitant to speak.

He reminded me of Solo, pausing for dramatic effect before explaining something.

"What?" I seethed, just loud enough for Guide not to overhear.

He looked surprised that I addressed him at all.

His eyes shifted suspiciously back and forth from me to Guide before responding.

"I'm looking for someone—" he began to plead. "My little sister."

Guide walked a few feet away to find a chair or something else to sit on while I worked.

He took the opportunity to continue talking, with her now out of the way.

The Hispanic boy with wild, dark curls implored, "I've been here for three months, and I know they brought my sister here, too, but I can never find out where she is. Please. She is four years old with long, soft, curly hair…like a baby doll. Her name is Rio. Please…please…have you seen her or heard of her at all?"

His face was long with anticipation and worry. I was sure if he could have gotten down on his knees to beg for information without getting in trouble, he would have.

I glanced at Guide, who had located an overturned painter's bucket to rest on. She didn't react as if she had heard any of our conversation.

You can't help everybody, but those you can help…you should.

Dani's words convicted me.

"Yeah, I know Rio," I breathed out, speaking in the same stealthy way I had picked up in the Laundry Center.

His face lit up, and he looked like he was about to explode with relief.

"Praise God Almighty in heaven!" he said a little too loudly for comfort, accidentally dropping his trowel into the wheelbarrow.

My eyes shot over at Guide again, but she still appeared unbothered by our exchange.

That made me nervous.

"Shhh..." I whispered harshly.

"Oh, sorry, sorry. Is she okay? Is she eating? Does she still have accidents?" the boy mumbled quickly, knowing he had to move back to the wall soon.

"She is okay. She is eating, and sometimes, she has accidents," I quietly answered just as rapidly.

His facial expression changed to discernable worry again, but he returned to the wall after retrieving his tool. I continued to stir the gray slop.

Rio had never mentioned having a brother, but she only talked about her parents once after her night terror, so it was plausible.

When it was time for him to collect more cement, he asked if Rio had difficulty adjusting to life at the TRP. That was irrelevant to me, but I told him she was enduring as best she could.

Curiosity finally got the better of me, so I asked, "What happened to your parents? She mentioned a fire."

He didn't show as much emotion as when asking about Rio's welfare, but he explained, "We were having bible study at our house when the Syndicate kicked in the door, shooting everyone that moved. I grabbed Rio, and we almost made it out the window when a soldier ripped her from my arms. I couldn't leave her behind, so I let them take me, too. They got me, Rio, and my oldest brother, then burned the house down with everyone else inside. We lost our parents and my younger brother. My name is Mateo, by the way."

"Raya," I offered in return. "I'm sorry for your loss."

"It's okay. They're in a better place now."

Mateo said it with such blind conviction as if he just knew.

"How can you be so calm about it? Death is horrible," I insisted.

"Death is a part of life. If you live right, why should you be afraid? We all have assurance in salvation and resurrection if we follow the Most High's commands and believe in the Messiah," he decreed matter-of-factly.

He walked away without warning, plastering the wall with the cement he had collected for his work section.

Just a few months ago, I said something similar to my brother in an argument. My words were coming back full circle.

I stood there in a daze of recollections.

Guide cleared her throat, snapping me back to reality, and I stirred the pile with the shovel.

Each time Mateo came to collect cement, he told me more about himself. He was my age, and his brother, Von, was twenty-one. They were brought from Tennessee.

In return, I told him a little about myself, but not much. I didn't trust a soul anymore.

The way Guide never intervened in our interaction made the hairs on the back of my neck stand up. This wasn't typical behavior for a hardened TRP guard.

"You remind me of this Ryan kid I knew," I randomly mentioned to Mateo, looking at his overgrown hair. "The last time I saw him, he needed a haircut, too."

"Well, if he is anything like me, he looks good with or without long hair," he bantered back.

I almost cracked a smile when I joked, "Sure...if you were a Syndicate soldier with shaggy auburn hair."

Guide stood up and shifted towards us, causing me to shut up immediately.

Mateo returned to work, helping the others patch the dents and holes in the wall.

Dark Shades finally appeared again, signaling that it was quitting time. She told Guide to take me back to M block, and she would ensure the boys returned to their barracks.

Guide nodded curtly.

When we entered the hallway, she pulled out a half-empty water bottle from her deep side pocket and offered it to me. Confused, I looked up in search of the cameras.

We were in a blind spot.

I glanced back at her and then down at the bottle.

Guide's left eye squinted slightly in annoyance, and she thrusted the bottle toward me again when I hesitated to take it.

My mouth began to water with the possibilities. Running my parched tongue across deeply cracked lips, I wanted to take it, but why was she offering it to me?

It was a lose-lose situation.

If I accepted it, I'd probably get into trouble, but if I didn't take it...

Insatiable thirst overpowered me, and I gave one last unsure glance at Guide before grasping for it. As soon as my fingers brushed the plastic container, searing pain exploded on the right side of my face. Guide had punched me.

My eye immediately began to swell shut.

She pushed me to the ground, grabbed the scruff of my collar, and dragged me down the hallway, choking me with the fabric along the way.

The water bottle rolled back and forth across the floor where it landed, making an eerie crinkling sound.

Another guard must have noticed when we came into full view of the camera because Karen ran up to her, all too eager to see me take three more days in the Chute.

"Another vacation from work is too good for this one—" Guide grumbled to Karen, who had pulled out her demerit device prematurely. "Nah...I'll deal with her my way."

This was the first time I had ever heard Guide speak.

Without further debate, she whisked me past Karen into a nearby lit broom closet and locked the door behind us.

Instead of the punches and kicks I braced myself for, she pulled me up and attentively dusted me off.

I cringed at her touch and scooted away. My heartbeat quickened when I looked up with my good eye and realized the room was void of cameras. I wanted to scream but knew better than to cause a scene.

I had no intentions of going back to the Chute.

"I'm sorry, but I had to. It was the only way to get you alone," Guide apologized while intentionally trying to approach me again.

I stepped further away from her, pressing my back to the wall in a weak attempt to distance myself more. With my nerves set on edge, I accidentally knocked a broomstick to the floor, causing a loud clanging noise.

She looked at me sincerely and explained, "My name is Marie. I have a son named Ryan. I lost him to the Syndicate. He has auburn hair like mine. He's eighteen. Is that the friend you were talking about?"

Her eyes pleaded for answers, but I was utterly speechless and confused, so I offered her no response. I couldn't be sure of someone who would offer me the means to punish me.

"Please, Raya. You have to trust me. I'm here to help. If you don't believe me, I can prove it. After dinner, go to the mess hall and tell Tiffany...the guard with the shades...that you need to help Bertha wash the dishes. Okay? You. Need. To. Help. Bertha. Wash. The. Dishes. Got that?"

Karen started knocking on the door, asking if Marie needed an assistant.

Marie quickly unlocked the door and grabbed me by the collar again, fully displaying my shut, swollen eye.

"I think we are good here," Marie boasted.

She held onto me the entire way to M block, pushing me towards the food line for all to see, and then disappeared.

At this point, I didn't know what to think. It was too much to comprehend, but I had nothing left for false promises and hope.

I retrieved my food tray and sat down to inhale the contents.

Shiri found me and gave me all of her food and half her water as well. I had no qualms in accepting the handout. I was beyond starved and relished the extra food and drink. A sister beside me pitied my incredible hunger and thirst. She slid me her entire water bottle, suggesting I save it for later.

After dinner, I walked in the slow-moving circle outside before entering my new cell home. I was astonished that I had the cell to myself, seeing that the TRP had an over-crowding issue, but maybe it was for the best that I was now alone.

Shiri was in the cell beside me and, after lights out, whispered how she and the other inmates had cared for Rio in my absence. She told me how they had crafted washable pull-ups out of donated socks for her.

I went to sleep, satisfied that I had made the right decision for Rio's sake but still very much concerned with the newfound unwelcome attention from Marie.

Twenty-Three

————— ◆ —————

Solo

"**I**'VE GOT THE COMPLETE layout. Well, pretty much. We just need a way to get there," I relayed to Juda. "I saw your sister on the cameras yesterday. I would be lying if I said she was okay. Man, everybody there looks like 'The Walking Dead'. It's crazy I didn't think to hack into their security feeds before. I was just so focused on too many things and nothing at all at the same time, you know what I mean?"

I paused out of habit, waiting for Juda to reply.

When he didn't, I told him my plans to create a temporary EMP to disable all the TRP's security measures when we arrived. We would still need to take inventory of how many weapons they had cached at the site.

I also didn't know how to create an electromagnetic pulse of energy that would specifically short-circuit no more than a five-mile radius. I needed to construct a superconductor to get the job done.

I had never put calculations that advanced into application before.

I told Juda I needed somewhere other than the Sanctuary to conduct my experiments in case something went left and I accidentally knocked out the power grid down here.

Deep in thought, I sat beside his bed and rubbed my sleepy eyes.

Mira had already come through to do her rounds and left but said she would return in a few hours. Adina was due back any minute, then I would go.

I promised I would meet Sheba in the training room to attempt our first run of the blindfolded mission. I would direct her through a miniature obstacle course to see how well we worked together.

I was actually looking forward to it.

Maybe if I told her my dilemma about the temporary EMP, she could provide a simple solution as she had done with the digital model of the TRP.

After Adina came in and began her daily checks and therapy for Juda, we shared some small talk. Then I told her I had to run.

Sheba was waiting impatiently for me in the training room. She was aggressively wrapping one of her headscarves into the shape of a blindfold when I got there.

"I thought you said 2:30. It's almost 3 PM," she balked at me.

"I was waiting for Adina to make it back to the Infirmary. We all agreed that my cousin needs round-the-clock care. I couldn't just leave him alone," I explained.

"Oh. My bad," she said, looking slightly ashamed that she had been impatient over something less pressing.

I told her it was all good and asked if she was ready to begin.

She looked nervous before suggesting I go first instead of her.

"I don't care either way. Sure. I'll go first," I barely managed to get out before she tied the blindfold over my eyes.

I could hear her walking away from me towards the entryway to the room; then she began with her instructions.

"Walk twenty paces slightly to your left. So, how is your cousin, anyway? The girl cousin, I mean," she started.

As I blindly walked to my left, my arms were outstretched to avoid blatantly running into something face first. I walked at a snail's pace, hoping not to trip or embarrass myself by falling.

"She isn't doing so great. I think they are retaliating against her for something. One guard dragged her down the hallway into a side room with no cameras the last time I saw her. She had a black eye when she came out," I rambled on while swinging my arms in front of me.

So far, I hadn't made any contact with anything.

"Stop. Now walk straight five paces, then turn around," Sheba instructed.

I did as I was told.

When I turned around, Sheba told me to walk ten paces to the left.

"What do you plan on doing about it?" she asked bluntly.

"Since I have a complete blueprint now, I just need to figure out how to implement a short-wave EMP. I can build a machine to cause one, but I can't do it here in the Sanctuary. It's too dangerous," I stated, forgetting about the pacing.

I stepped one pace too far and stubbed my toe on a dumbbell.

"You overstepped. You aren't listening to me," Sheba chided. "Step one pace to the right, then straight fifteen steps."

After rubbing my foot, I moved to the right and went straight.

"What's an EMP? Why is it dangerous?" she continued to question.

I explained to her that it was an electromagnetic pulse meant to disable power, security, and any other battery-operated device altogether. I told her if I made a mistake and it went off down here, we could lose the ability to breathe clean air, among other things.

"Stop. You're where you need to be," she blurted out suddenly.

I took off the blindfold and stood in front of the punching bag. A note taped to it read, "I trust you."

I looked over at Sheba, standing at the doorway with her arms folded while leaning against the frame. She was smiling at the completion of her own smug game.

"You have those storage boulders. Can't you build it in one of those?"

"Sheba, I'm not so sure I'm the most intelligent person in the room anymore. That's literally THE answer!" I marveled wide-eyedly at her.

She shrugged like it was no big deal.

"I have my moments, I guess," she reservedly answered.

I didn't get the chance to reply before I heard my name echoing throughout the hallway. It was Adina calling out to me.

She was breathless by the time she became visible to us. Her tear-filled eyes and the glinting white of her toothy smile filled my gut with hopeful butterflies.

"Solo—" she crooned my name in a whispery half laugh, half cry. "It's Juda...he's awake. Come quick!"

Without hesitation, I took off down the tunnel back to the Infirmary, with Adina quick on my heels, leaving Sheba alone.

I reached the Infirmary just as Mira gently pulled out the tube that went down into Juda's stomach through his nose. I lingered in the doorway, not knowing what to do with myself. I gasped at the sudden feel of Adina's reassuring grip on my shoulder. She looked up at me and smiled before entering the room, causing Mira to look up.

"Look who's here," Mira announced, but I wasn't sure if she was directing that to me or Juda.

He coughed after the tube was removed, and it was hands down the best sound I had ever heard come out of my cousin's mouth.

Juda looked at me blankly as if trying to fit me like a puzzle piece into his memories but couldn't quite make the connection.

After everything we'd been through together, it seemed that he had forgotten me.

"It's me, Solo. Solomon. Your cousin," I insisted, pleading for him to remember.

Juda opened his mouth to speak, but the only sound that came out was a hoarse rasp. He looked like a fish gulping for air.

"Take it easy, Juda," Adina cautioned. "It may take a few days for your throat to heal fully. You had the tube in for a long while."

Juda stared at Adina like a child would his teacher as she taught a new concept, but he nodded briefly in understanding.

I entered the room and sat beside Juda in the hard plastic chair that occupied the walkway beside his bed.

I reached for his hand, and when he didn't resist, I squeezed it and beamed my sincerest smile at him.

Praise the Father!

"It's a true miracle, Juda. Praise the Most High...you're awake! You don't know how long I waited for this, man," I stammered excitedly.

Even though Adina told him to take it easy, he still tried to rasp out words. He moved his mouth, but nothing coherent came out; only the sound of forced air exited his lips.

Adina and Mira gave each other knowing looks and excused themselves from the room, leaving me alone with him.

"Are you hungry? Thirsty? I can go get you something from the kitchen," I rapidly asked, trying to ensure that he was comfortable.

He shook his head 'no'.

I could tell that he was getting frustrated and over-stimulated.

He desperately wanted to speak.

Juda tried his voice repeatedly with no luck until he could finally breathe out one word...one name.

"Raya..."

Twenty-Four

8 AM. Monday.

Marie stood beside me with her AR-15 while I waited in the laundry line.

Dark Shades walked up to her and whispered something in her ear.

I couldn't read her lips, so I studied her face while she leaned into Marie's personal space. I couldn't get over the fact that her name was Tiffany. It made her sound human and didn't fit well with her current phony personality.

Marie nudged me to get out of line. I was going back to the wall to stir cement today.

Shiri shot me a worried look as I walked away, but I tried to give her an appearance of reassurance, even with the swollen eye.

Dark Shades led the way again.

When we got to the outside alcove, Mateo was there, and his face lit up when he saw me. Without caring that Dark Shades or Marie was standing there, he greeted me and asked what happened to my eye.

Marie looked at me sternly, encouraging my silence.

"I ran into a wall," I insisted while touching the sore spot.

"Right..." he returned, clearly noting that I was lying. "How's my sister doing? Did you see her yesterday?"

I was thankful for the change of subject.

"I didn't see her yesterday, but another inmate told me that everyone is looking out for her now. She will be okay," I told him, still uncomfortable that Marie and Dark Shades were standing within earshot.

Marie found her overturned bucket again and took her place of observation while Dark Shades went wherever Dark Shades usually went.

I stirred the cement, not looking forward to another rerun of yesterday.

When Mateo came to collect a scoop of wet cement, he told me to trust Marie.

My face contorted in skepticism, so he explained, "She is one of us. She was forced into service by the Commander of the Syndicate. She is on our side."

While his words tried to penetrate my principles, my logic didn't want to believe that someone like her could be on my side. She gave demerits. She mindlessly went along with all of this foolishness.

She hit me.

"I think I'm good on all of that, Mateo. But if you want, I can get a message to Rio. Anything you want to tell her?" I responded.

"Yeah," he smirked. "Tell her good night, good night..."

I thought that was weird, but shrugged and agreed to pass the message when I could.

"I hope you change your mind about Marie. If she told you to wash the dishes...you should at least try," he challenged.

He went back to the wall and continued his work. When I focused on the alcove, I could tell the repairs were almost complete. I assumed that this would be the last time I ever saw Mateo.

In my thoughts, I weighed the pros and cons of listening to him and trusting Marie.

She said that she was Ryan's mom.

What if she is telling the truth?

When Mateo returned, he didn't appear to have any intentions of conversing with me, but I had to know.

"Is Marie an engineer?"

"Yeah, she is the one they call to design repair plans when something breaks down or fails here," he laughingly said. "But every 'repair' she makes weakens the TRP structure. Like this wall. Putting cement on it is gonna make it crumble apart quicker. It's actually kinda funny if you think about it."

I didn't see the humor in it.

I looked over at Marie, and she was scrutinizing my every move. If she really was Ryan's mom, I owed it to her to tell her what happened to her son.

My brain felt like it was going to rip in half.

I didn't know what to do, and I was done praying.

I couldn't.

Whatever they did to me in the Chute was sticking.

Those chants sprung forth, overtaking my mental space whenever I tried to pray.

It was useless.

I wasn't sure where my faith had retreated to, but it was shaken.

I stirred every few minutes for hours until Dark Shades came out the door and told Marie it was time to head back.

The repair was complete, and Mateo gave me a weak smile goodbye as Dark Shades led them away back to their block.

As Marie guided me back to M block, I held my head down to avoid her gaze.

I wasn't going to fall for any more of her tricks today.

At an intersection of hallways, another inmate was about to cross our path, pushing a food cart with covered trays. She tried going past us, expecting us to yield to her, but when Marie defiantly stepped in her path, she had to stop abruptly. Before she stopped, she ran into my right side with the cart, causing one of the trays to slide off and splatter onto the ground.

It appeared to be filled with a sizable slice of chocolate cake and a paper cup full of coffee. The remains of the cake were splayed out all over the floor, and the coffee, still steaming hot, followed suit.

My hip was on fire from the sudden strike, and I couldn't help reaching down to rub the pain away. When I looked up to apologize for getting in the way, the other inmate had closed the gap between us and reached for my throat.

Her hands gripped my neck tightly, choking me in a blind rage.

It happened so fast that I was too shocked to respond in defense right away. I stood there, unable to breathe or comprehend that the person trying to kill me was Naomi.

My hands reached out to grip her arms instinctively, and I finally dug my jagged nails into her veins, drawing blood.

She shrieked in pain and let go of my neck but quickly moved to scratch my face.

Marie must have been just as shocked by Naomi's reaction because she hesitated to do anything at first.

When she finally came to her senses, she extended her baton and forcefully struck Naomi across the left side of her head, drawing more blood. Naomi automatically reached for her ear and withdrew from me.

Marie pointed the AR-15 at Naomi's face and, without saying it, motioned for her to get down on the ground.

Naomi put her hands in the air and complied, stretching out on the ground.

Karen showed up with Miss just as Marie put zip ties around Naomi's wrists.

"And just what do you think you are doing, Marie? This one was bringing me my dinner. Let her up this instant," Miss harped, seeming to have made Naomi her personal pet.

Marie picked Naomi up from the ground by her arms, which were still tied behind her back.

"It was probably that troublemaker's fault," Karen added, glaring in my direction as she pulled out her demerit device.

Miss glanced at Karen in disdain.

"Put that thing away," Miss clucked and smiled wickedly at me.

She motioned for Marie to continue taking me back to my barracks and then told Karen to cut Naomi loose so she could clean up her mess.

Miss coddled Naomi briefly and petted her head before Naomi bent down to swipe the splattered cake into a pile with her hands.

I wanted to throw up watching their interaction.

At least I didn't catch a demerit.

As we walked away, I heard Miss telling Karen that they needed to discuss her new work assignment on K block. Karen seemed genuinely taken aback that she was being made to relocate.

I smiled inwardly.

No more dreaded Tuesdays in the Laundry Center.

I couldn't wait to tell Shiri.

Twenty-Five

—— ⚜ ——

8 AM. Tuesday.

Shiri stood behind me in our work line and whispered, "Are you sure she is gone? Like gone, gone?"

"Yep," I croaked out, concerning the absence of Karen.

My hip, heavily bruised from Naomi's cart, left me with a slight limp.

I was almost glad that there were no mirrors here.

Surely, I looked like a pegged-leg pirate by now with one eye hooded and a limping gait.

Sensing my self-consciousness, Shiri decreed, "You look great, Captain Raya...arghh."

She hooked her pointer finger at me while she said it in a pirate's accent.

I almost laughed out loud, forgetting where we were for a blissful moment.

Shiri knew me better than I knew myself sometimes.

"I've been praying for you, Raya. I know experiencing the Chute is not easy on the mind. I've seen some people return mentally broken and never make it back to themselves. The fact that you still have it in you to laugh or talk is amazing," she commended.

I didn't feel amazing, but I thanked her for the prayers. At least someone was praying on my behalf.

Marie showed up a little later than expected, and her movements portrayed that she was frazzled, but steadfast to her charade, she never spoke.

She walked us to the Laundry Center and closed the door once we entered. As usual, Marie waited outside.

I needed to unburden myself of everything I knew. I decided to take a chance and trust Shiri with all that I had learned, so I laid it all out on her.

Since Karen was no longer watching our cameras, it took me eight hours, but I got Shiri up to speed on everything that had gone on with me, who Marie said she was, and meeting Rio's brother.

"Sis, we need to wash the dishes then," she simply said after I had released it all onto her.

"You think so? She hit me," I responded while putting my hand up to my eye. "How can I trust her when she hit me?"

Shiri chuckled a little under her breath at my simpleness.

"She did it to get you alone. Why can't you let it go?"

I reflected on her words briefly, still holding a slight grudge for being punched without provocation.

"Fine. We can wash the dishes after dinner. I need to see Rio. Can you get a message to her to come wash dishes with us?" I asked.

"Of course. She's been asking for you nonstop and misses you like crazy. She told me to tell you that she was sorry for getting you in trouble, but I told her that you were okay," Shiri comforted.

As she spoke, a rush of emotion stormed through my body. I hadn't realized just how much I missed the little girl until this very moment.

Marie opened the door to let us out after our shift, and as I passed her, I thought I caught a glimpse of pleading in her eyes. My facial expressions conveyed indifference in return. I didn't want her to have the satisfaction of knowing that she would soon get what she wanted.

Shiri ate dinner with Rio a few tables away from me. I knew better than to approach Rio directly, but I watched them as they conversed. Rio's smile lit up the room along with my heart, after Shiri told her that she would get to see me again while we 'washed the dishes'.

When it was time to go outside, I waited a few minutes until most of the other sisters piled outside to walk on their imaginary hamster's wheel. Shiri, holding Rio's baby hand, scooted over to the mess hall counter where Dark Shades stood guard. She looked towards me, and I knew that was my cue to join them. I swiftly exited my seat and took my tray to the counter. Behind Dark Shades, the door was obscured by a heavy-set woman, who I had to assume was Bertha. She clutched a dish towel, preparing to clear all the food trays.

"Um, we need to help Bertha wash the dishes?" I said more in question form, still unsure what to expect from this encounter. It could have all been one extensive setup, and I was playing the fool, dragging Shiri and Rio down with me.

Dark Shades took off her sunglasses and sized us up one by one. I noticed that her eyes were a dull shade of green. She looked mixed, but who was I to say for sure.

She nudged her chin in the direction of the mini kitchen, and Bertha stepped out of our way as we entered.

"Y'all trying to wash the dishes, huh?" the heavy-set woman inquired while wiping out a gray tray. "Well, come on then."

She grunted because of her knees while bending down, swirling open the large air duct vent across from the sink. It was big enough for us to fit one at a time.

Shiri looked into the dark hole, shrugged her shoulders as if to say, 'might as well', got down on all fours, and crawled in without further questioning.

Rio followed suit.

On the other hand, I broke out into a cold sweat, recalling the confining space of the Chute. I started to panic, staring at the opening, breathing in quick, shallow breaths.

"It's okay, child. Washing the dishes can heal what you've got going on," Bertha calmly stated while winking and brushing my arms with her rough hands. "Just follow your friends. It's not too long a distance. You'll be just fine."

I took a deep, calming breath and exhaled loudly, mentally declaring that I could and would do this.

I stooped down and entered the vent.

It took a few seconds, but my eyes adjusted to the darkness, and I could see Rio's little body moving quickly ahead of me. I crawled faster to catch up with her. It did feel better knowing someone else was nearby, and after about five minutes of meandering straight through the stifling vent, a light began to break forth ahead of Shiri.

She stopped at the end of the grate, causing me and Rio to stop behind her. The grate wasn't bolted shut, so she easily swung it open and crawled into a vast room that housed several HVAC systems. They were all lining the walls and humming softly from use. Although the room was larger, it was stuffier than the vents.

After I freed myself of the tight space, I saw that about ten other inmates spread themselves throughout the room, along with Marie.

They were both male and female.

I searched the room for Mateo, and to my relief, he was talking to another older boy, who looked very similar, in a corner. When they both caught sight of the tiny girl with oversized clothes crawling into the room, they rushed to her and hugged her in a big collective squeeze. The other young man must have been his older brother, Von. Rio was giggling in excitement at being reunited with her older brothers.

Mateo, especially, carried a strong sense of brotherly affection towards Rio. He barely put her down when Marie called for everyone's attention. She asked that everyone have a seat.

"Okay, we don't have much time today. I received some news, but first, let us welcome our three newcomers, Raya,

Shiri, and Rio," she began, putting her hands together like a teacher introducing new students to the class.

I was kind of shocked that she knew all our names, and even the sound of her voice threw me off since she never spoke to anyone while playing the role of a guard.

She continued after everyone silently acknowledged us with head nods or blank stares, "We are going to have to move up our timeline if this plan is going to work. I've just been told that Tiffany and I will be relocated to Transcendent- Seattle at the end of the year, so we only have one more expected shipment of weapons to glean from. I'm not sure if that will be enough, but we have got to at least try."

Is she talking about an escape plan?

"I think we can do it. With the Most High, all things are possible," Mateo chimed in while staring at Rio, then looking over at me.

He was still in awe that he had finally been reunited with his beloved sister. He gripped her tightly in a brotherly hug and didn't appear to have any intentions of letting her go again. My mind immediately jumped to Juda, and my heart sank like a capsized boat.

I would never get to embrace him like that or play fight with him or joke around or argue with him.

That darkness within started to creep up and consume me. I bowed my head, not wanting to be gawked at as I descended into my feelings. I felt Shiri's arm interlock with mine. She knew me and knew that I was in a bad way even without me having to verbalize it.

"Before we go over the plan, let's take a few prayer requests and praise the Most High in song," Marie entreated.

Shiri's hand shot up in the air.

"You don't have to raise your hand. It's okay to speak freely here," Marie insisted.

Shiri put her hand down slowly in embarrassment before requesting, "Raya was in the Chute for two days. Can we please pray for her?"

Marie nodded.

"Anyone else?"

A middle-aged, skinny man spoke up and asked that we all pray for his son. He wasn't sure what happened to him when they were first brought to the TRP months ago, but he wanted to pray for his safety.

I stared at Marie while he spoke and read her facial expressions.

Dad always taught Juda and me to pay special attention to what a person wasn't saying by taking note of their body language. Non-verbal cues rarely ever lied, unlike people.

Marie knew something about the man's son.

That much was apparent by the subtle grimaces on her face, but she didn't offer any information that would likely put his mind at ease. I wondered at her reasoning for withholding information from someone she seemed to trust.

Another prayer request was made for family and friends who were still relatively free on the outside...ones they may never see again in this lifetime.

Marie, still standing, walked to one of the heating units and reached behind it, struggling to free something.

Eventually, she pulled out a wad of faded pink and green bandanas. She handed them out to all the females in the room so we could cover our heads during prayer.

Von stood up and prayed according to everyone's request. His speech was shaky with emotion, thanking the Father fervently for allowing him to reunite with his remaining family members. He prayed for my mind to be stayed on Him and to loose whatever strongholds the enemy had gained over me in my time of torture. He prayed safety for all the loved ones who were separated physically and spiritually, asking for the Most High to open doorways of opportunity to seek comfort and sanctuary in Him. It was a powerful yet quick prayer.

Afterward, Shiri stood up and sang the Shema[1].

I closed my eyes and listened to her smooth voice rise and fall as she repeated the credo. Her voice didn't compare to Chava's but had the same inward frisson effect.

She sang like how being at home, in peace and fully protected, felt.

After she finished, she sat back down on the dusty gray tiled floor. Marie thanked her for her beautiful rendition of the Shema, then returned to business regarding the escape plan.

Marie explained, more so to Shiri and me, that they had been planning to overtake the TRP by coup for months. They were taking one or two guns from their weapons shipments and hiding them in this utility room connected to all the blocks. Marie was nervous that Miss suspected her or Tiffany of skimming off the top for their own personal gain, and that's why they were both being relocated.

"We were supposed to have enough weapons to overtake the snipers and the guards that aren't loyal to the cause by next March. I'm afraid we've run out of time," Marie said, glancing at her wristwatch. "We will meet again in two days, and we can discuss this further."

---

1. "Hear (shema), O Israel: The Lord our God is one Lord." (Deut. 6:4)

Everyone quickly got up and went toward their respective vent doors. Mateo leaned down, gave Rio a long kiss on the forehead, and softly said, "Good night, good night…"

To which Rio responded gladly, "Construction site."

He let her go, knowing that now he had hopes of seeing her again in a few days.

Rio moved towards me and silently reached out for my hand. I took her hand and smiled lovingly down at her before we turned to go through our vent, marked with an M.

Before I could stoop down to exit the room, Marie walked over to me and grabbed my free arm.

"Raya. Wait. Please."

I turned to Shiri, and she heedfully understood to take Rio through without me.

I would follow them shortly.

"My son. Ryan. Please, tell me what you know," she pleaded desperately.

"He is okay, I think," I responded carefully, still not knowing if I should trust this woman.

If I got on the wrong side by telling her what Ryan did to save me, she could make my life worse in spite.

"What do you mean? Listen, I'm sorry I hit you. I couldn't figure out any other way to speak to you privately. I needed to know about my son. Please," she begged.

I sighed, forgiving her in my heart.

"He was with me and my family for a few months before I was brought here. The Syndicate shot him in the back when he tried to save me. I think he is okay, but I'm not 100% certain," I blurted out.

Her face fell into a worried mother's expression. She seemed to be calculating something silently to herself.

"How did he end up with you?" she asked in a rush.

I explained that he was a Syndicate soldier who defected on one of their missions to a Hebrew wedding...that he helped a group of us by turning his weapon on his fellow soldiers. I told her that he asked to come with us then helped us learn about the Syndicate and their combat tactics.

She closed her eyes and sighed deeply in solace.

"Praise the Most High," Marie whispered.

"I have a question for you now. Why aren't you telling the whole truth to everyone?" I boldly questioned.

She looked confused before I explained, "I can see it written all over your face. People are looking for their loved ones, and you have information. Why aren't you sharing it?"

She looked like she had been caught in a snare.

"I can't. We will never be able to escape this place without hope. If people knew what became of their loved ones, they would lose hope and give up. You need to leave. You don't have any more time left. Hurry."

She pushed me towards the vent in her guard-like manner.

"I'll explain more on Thursday. Just please go. Now," she barked.

I entered the gloomy vent, rushing to return to the other side. I didn't have time for my nerves to get the best of me while alone in the dark, cramped space.

When I plunged out the grate, Bertha was wringing her hands together and pacing back and forth.

"Finally! Chile...I thought we was caught for sho," she said as she again blocked the doorway leading out to the common area.

She turned around and walked out, motioning for me to follow.

"Lights out!" a female guard shouted from down the corridor. "What are you two doing back there?!"

The guard began walking our way with her truncheon posed and ready to swing.

All the other M block inmates were in their cells, watching in quiet suspense.

I peered down the aisle and saw Shiri standing with her face against the bars, looking to see what my fate would be.

"Oh, oh, we real sorry, ma'am. I spilled a pot of grease all over the floor and it took a little longer to get it up. Even with her help," Bertha stammered out.

The guard used the raised baton to point back toward our empty cells, "Well! On with it! *Lazy, good-for-nothing roaches.*"

She whispered the ending insult loudly but made no move to give out any demerits.

Once I entered my cell, I let go of the breath I was unconsciously holding and lay in my bunk with a loud thud.

Shiri didn't try speaking to me, and I was grateful.

I needed to reign in all my racing thoughts.

Marie may be on to something about hope, but how can I help us escape...

TWENTY-SIX

—— ⬦ ——

5 PM. THURSDAY.

Dinner was over, and I hastily delivered my food tray to Bertha. Shiri and Rio were, again, behind me.

"We need to help Bertha wash the dishes," I articulated quickly to Dark Shades.

I was anxious to get through the vent and into the hot room with the heating systems.

I needed to speak to Marie about her flawed plans.

I had two days of calculating revisions to what she said. Planning all the previously successful rescue missions had prepared me for strategizing, and I was impatient to share suggestions with everyone.

Dark Shades begrudgingly allowed us in, and Bertha swung open the vent grate. She smiled at me but held me back before I could crawl in.

"Don't stay too long. I can't keep making excuses," she warned.

"Yes, ma'am," I conceded.

I entered the vent quickly and held my breath for as long as I could stand, hoping I didn't panic from voluntarily entering the tight space again.

By the time we reached the end, I was out of breath and gulped down the hot air in the room like my fate depended on it.

I hated the vent.

If it weren't the only means of transport to the secret meetings, I would never enter it again.

Marie and twelve others were waiting in the room this time.

I didn't pay much attention to the block letters patched into their uniforms two days ago, but I paid careful attention today.

Everything depended on it.

Marie rushed to begin, knowing less than an hour was available to us.

"Von, do you mind praying us in again?" she questioned.

She retrieved the bandanas and passed them out, but we were short one.

"It's okay," Shiri offered, "We can share."

She and I held our heads close together and stretched the bandana across our two crowns.

Von cleared his throat then began his prayer. It was clear and concise, but most importantly, it was uplifting.

Rio had snuggled into her brother's lap, leaning on him and playing with his uniform's buttons while her oldest brother prayed.

After the prayer, we got right to business.

Marie gave us all the logistics of weaponry available and the breakdown of what we were actually up against.

"There are one hundred and thirty soldiers on premise, with five assigned to each of the twenty-six blocks. We rotate shifts for the security camera room, and there is always one in the bird's nest overlooking each block. That leaves three soldiers guarding inmates at all times. We have ten additional floaters who fill in where needed, like at the gate or the Intake Center. I have ten implant agents of my own that are sympathetic to our cause. I cannot tell you who they are, so please don't ask. I will not jeopardize their lives or yours. Recently, an inmate knew too much about a head organizer operating on the outside, and now reports are circulating that she has been captured and the inmate 'released'."

Marie paused a second and looked down distraughtly at the floor. She must have known this woman personally and was deeply affected by her capture.

She quickly gathered herself and continued, "Right...we have access to fifteen handguns and five rifles right now, with another shipment coming in two weeks. My implants each have their own service weapon, but it's not enough. I aimed to outfit at least two people from each block to assist in taking down the non-compliant soldiers. And then there is Miss Agatha..."

She visibly shuddered at the mere mention of the name.

Mateo spoke up first, "If we don't have enough weapons, maybe we can make weapons out of other things like food trays or something."

Marie nodded slowly, mulling the idea over.

"Can we back up a second? Maybe I didn't hear the part where these soldiers would all be in the same place for us to overtake them. Or are we supposed to hope that each block takes down their guards at the same exact time?" Shiri skeptically threw out.

The room got quiet for a few moments while everyone thought about the repercussions of bad timing.

"I have an idea," I declared into the silence.

Everyone looked at me in anticipation.

I could hear whispers of rumors circulating regarding what I did to that guard.

I had no idea that my actions were spoken of outside of M block or how that information even leaked out.

"An assembly. We need another assembly. That way, all the inmates and guards are in the yard together, and we can switch on them simultaneously," I suggested.

Again, there was silence for a few seconds.

"That's actually a great idea, Raya," Von ventured. "But how are we gonna get Miss to call an assembly? She just gave out coats, and the only way another assembly would be called is for a public execution."

"Then we have a public execution," Mateo replied matter-of-factly. "I volunteer."

The murmurs kicked into high gear then.

"Okay, settle down, please. Raya, did you have more to this theory before we have martyrs on our hands?" Marie questioned while glaring at Mateo, clearly not in agreement with his outburst.

I looked around the group and memorized their block letters.

"Yeah. You said we don't have enough weapons or participants from the looks of it, but we can change that. During the last assembly, I saw members of my church in some of the blocks. I'm sure y'all saw people you knew, too. If we play our cards right, we can get messages to those we know and trust through each other. Then, have them pass messages to those they trust in their block. We outnumber the guards seven to one. We can overtake them without that many weapons if we have the numbers willing to turn on them," I elaborated.

Shiri looked like she was making her own calculations with her eyes centered on the ceiling before she interjected.

"Then you're gonna need D and E block the most. They both take shifts in the kitchen and transport the food trays to all the other female blocks. They can carry messages all throughout the female barracks. What are the kitchen blocks for the males?" Shiri asked the room.

A middle-aged man spoke up, "Q and R. I'm on R."

Shiri nodded her head and gave a crazed smile, "Yes...it can work if we have the kitchen blocks on our side. They are the rumor spreaders. But we will need to be careful. A few individuals in D block will betray us in a heartbeat."

Shiri looked down at my injured hip, which was starting to heal.

My limp was becoming less noticeable, but it was still a daily reminder that Naomi was not to be trusted.

Marie rubbed her chin in contemplation and paced the floor.

"This could work...this could really work," she muttered to herself. "I can put my people in the sniper's towers. Well, most of them. They can take out the other snipers. The inmates can overtake the guards quickly and strip them of their weapons if we time everything down to the minute. We could lock the remaining soldiers up until we all escape."

"There are still some other details we need to work out. Like transportation. Say all this works. How are we gonna escape here? What about Miss? She isn't exactly a predictable variable," a female from H block stated sarcastically.

I did a double-take at her.

It was the same light-skinned girl who worked the third shift at the Laundry Center. She looked angry or zealous about something when she passed me the first time in the hallway, and she had that same glower on her face now.

"Don't be a doubting Thomas[1] , Leah," Von scolded. "We have a little time. Everything will fall into place according to the Most High's will and glory."

"I never said I didn't have faith. Not sure where that came from, but this is life or death. They will execute all of us if this doesn't work exactly how it needs to," Leah retorted.

Von, nor anyone else, refuted her statement.

Marie checked her wristwatch and told everyone it was time to go.

---

1. John 20: 24-29

We would meet again on Saturday.

Rio ran into my arms after Mateo and Von hugged her and said their special goodbyes. I picked her up and balanced her on my good hip.

"You're heavy, young lady," I said to her before putting her down and reaching for her hand instead.

She giggled and shined a brilliant babyish smile at me. Her cuteness was too much, and my heart melted.

Everything I had planned, the reason I felt alive again, was all because of her. She had no business being in this situation, and I would stop at nothing to get her out.

I praised the Most High with a quick prayer for placing her in my life.

After I finished my silent prayer, I realized that the chantings were no longer hijacking my thoughts, blocking me from reaching out to God.

Praise You, Father, infinitely, above all.

We all had much to think about for the next two days, but I felt up to the task as we crawled back through the vents.

"Come on, let's hurry. We don't need another close call like the other day," Shiri said, her voice reverberating off the hollow metal walls of the vent.

We picked up the pace and came out the other side just as Bertha was stacking the last of the gray trays onto a rolling food cart.

She breathed a sigh of relief at the sight of us and put her right hand across her heart.

"Every time. Every time. It never gets less nerve-wracking," Bertha exclaimed, more so to herself than us.

We thanked her for letting us help her with the dishes, and Shiri and Rio walked out of the mini kitchen.

I waited a minute to give them distance so it wasn't as apparent that we were all together.

We cautiously crept to our respective cells and tucked in for the night.

"Good night, bestie," I whispered to Shiri.

"Night, lady," she returned.

Even though her words were brief, I could hear the hope in them.

TWENTY-SEVEN

SOLO

"I'LL BE GONE FOR a few days, but Adina and Big Man will be checking on you while I'm away," I explained to a more alert Juda.

He was still confined to the med room but had more waking hours than resting, which was a significant improvement, according to Mira. He was also gaining his speech back slowly but had no use of his legs yet.

Adina made him drink the Willow tea religiously, fearing that the chemicals were still circulating throughout his blood. She wanted to proactively avoid any reversions or seizures.

I clutched my oversized backpack to my shoulder, nervously awaiting his response. I had gotten so used to our one-sided conversations that it was still surprising to hear his hoarse voice addressing me.

"Be—" he rasped slowly, not wanting to damage his vocal cords further. "—Careful. Please."

"I will. It's just a few days. Hopefully, I'll have the EMP device ready in just a couple of days. Raya is getting a plan together on her side, too. Once we know the day of their planned coup, we can move out and shut that place down once and for all. She is gonna be okay, Juda. Don't worry."

He shook his head slowly.

"Worried. About—" Juda breathed while pointing in my direction. "—You."

"Worried about me? I'm fine. Great," I countered.

"I. Heard. You," he mumbled while staring deep into my soul.

He folded his arms like he anticipated an explanation, but I had nothing to give him.

I wanted to put everything behind me and move forward in peace and well-being.

After I awkwardly said nothing, he cleared his throat and grunted, "You. Are. Enough. Solo. You...are always enough, man."

I nodded like an idiot and turned to leave so he couldn't see the emotion behind my eyes.

All the failures and inadequacies I held onto for the past few weeks were starting to melt away and seemed so irrelevant now.

As I walked out of the Infirmary, Sheba saw me in the tunnel and started to move my way.

"Wassup? You headed off somewhere?" she happily asked, bouncing on her heels.

"Yeah…I'm gonna go build that device I told you about. I'll be back in a few days," I answered curtly.

I started walking to my right, down the entrance tunnel.

It was late Thursday evening, and I would have the cover of night on my side to get to one of the spare storage boulders without being detected.

I aimed to complete the EMP by Shabbat, but I had enough provisions with me in case that didn't work out.

"I hear it's a three-mile walk this way. You want some company?" she asked, but it seemed like no matter the answer, she planned on coming anyway.

She was walking in step with me and swaying side to side nervously.

"Um, I don't think that's a good idea, Sheba. People might start to talk," I answered.

"Talk about what? We're just friends," she challenged.

"Exactly. Look, I appreciate the gesture and all, but I can manage by myself, and people need to see that all we are is just friends. Like you said," I explained politely, hoping that would appease her.

She shrugged and decreed, "Okay. Yeah. Sure. Fine. Good luck."

She seemed determined to be affronted, but I wasn't gonna back down this time.

She turned and walked awkwardly down the opposite direction towards the exit tunnel, kicking at the ground as she went.

I frowned at the back of her silhouette, then gave a dismissive shrug. I wouldn't worry about babying Sheba's feelings right now.

Too much was at stake.

I walked the three-mile tunnel, going over schematics and equations in my head. I was aiming for an EMP that would disable the facility for no more than thirty minutes. That's all we needed if Raya pulled off her end of the coup.

Walking alone, I realized how eerily quiet it was in the tunnel, even with my thoughts occupying me. I pulled out my headphones and phablet from my backpack to listen to music and pass the time. I found my favorite classic, 'Gotta Be New' by Isaiah Parah, and put it on repeat.

In less than thirty minutes, I was exiting the Sanctuary into the night.

Taking off my headphones, I replaced them with my night vision glasses and checked my surroundings while crouching as close to the ground as possible. I saw nothing approaching, but I took out a Bowie knife just in case I had to protect myself.

To get to the empty storage boulder, I would have to get pretty close to the pond, and that knowledge made my palms clammy and my stomach queasy from nervousness.

Since the old house was being used as a full-blown Syndicate base, there were bound to be soldiers patrolling nearby in the woods.

I prayed to God that I didn't encounter any of them on my way.

I crept as silently as possible through the dense woods for the quarter-mile trek toward the pond, but my high tops still rustled leaves along the way.

I picked up infrared lighting of soldiers' body heat a few times but quickly maneuvered out of their path. Nearing the storage boulder unscathed, I could see two thermal readings of soldiers propped up against it, laughing and joshing with each other.

I squatted and waited for them to leave, but after twenty minutes of listening to their cackling, I had to devise an alternate plan to get them away from the area.

Rummaging quietly through my backpack, I pulled out an old wristwatch with a timed alarm. Standing up and covertly walking forty paces south of the men, I set the timer so that in five minutes, it would sound a loud alarm. Then I strapped the watch to a small tree limb.

I hustled back to my original spot and kneeled closely to the cold ground, almost hugging it.

Precisely five minutes later, the watch went off in a horrendous shrill, causing the men to jump up and skirt, guns drawn, towards the squawking.

I dashed from my position to the boulder, typed in the code at the hidden keypad near the bottom, and slid under the opening, careful not to knock off as much of the dirt and debris accumulated on it.

I needed my hiding place to look as natural and camouflaged as possible.

Once inside, I listened for the soldiers' return, and when it did not come, I turned on the flashlight feature to my glasses. They illuminated the space quite well, which I would need for the duration of my stay.

I designed the storage boulders, and the inside was soundproof and insulated. No one would be able to see or hear my tinkering, but I would be able to listen to them clearly.

The boulder was almost as tall as me and wide enough for what I needed. The space suited my needs just fine.

I pulled out my supplies, organized them by relevance, and got to work.

Twenty-Eight

Raya

5 PM. Saturday.

As soon as everyone entered the basement utility room for the underground meeting, Marie asked that everyone recite their favorite scripture quickly in commemoration of the Sabbath, even though it ended within minutes.

I hadn't thought about Shabbat in such a long time; I had almost gotten used to not observing it.

That realization made guilt bloom in my stomach, and shame shiver down my spine.

I was glad that I was almost last to recite.

I had to remember the wording of the scripture I wanted to convey, and all my thoughts were jumbling together.

Shiri recited Titus 3:9, and when it was my turn, I fumbled out 2 Peter 3:18.

"But grow in grace, and in the knowledge of our Lord and Saviour Christ. To him be glory both now and for ever. Amen."

Hearing all the other recited scriptures helped my detached sense of self that I had reluctantly acquired in the Chute. It was like therapy for my underlying depression, a balm to my well-being and soul.

Afterwards, we got straight to the plan.

"How will we secure the gate?" Mateo asked.

"A better question is how are you gonna volunteer to be executed when you are too compliant as is? You don't even have a single demerit yet, and we've been here for months," Von criticized his little brother jokingly.

Mateo smirked at him and replied, "I can be a handful if I wanna be."

"But seriously, it needs to be someone more believable. Someone like me," Von replied, emphasizing himself by touching his chest.

His posture and general body language did speak to him being of a more rebellious nature than his brother.

Everyone looked to agree with their whispered consents, then focused on Marie to see if she was with it. She nodded and said that it made her no difference as long as it happened smoothly.

"We have to be extremely careful with this information. If it gets into the wrong hands, everything we've worked towards will be for nothing, and many of you will pay the price. So for this message system to work, it must be by word of mouth only, understood?' Marie proposed.

Everyone nodded in agreement.

Rio had fallen fast asleep in Mateo's arms, and I was glad she wouldn't hear the next part of our discussion.

"How will we get the weapons to each block?" I asked, hoping Marie had a more detailed answer than the last time we discussed it.

Marie's voice was quiet yet tense.

"With the twenty weapons we already have stored, when the shipment comes November 25th, which is a Sunday, we can skim six more handguns and implement the plan the same day, or we can skim two guns and wait a few days until the proverbial dust settles. If we take six, Miss will notice immediately. We would have to take her out the same day."

There was a few seconds of calculated silence amongst the fourteen of us inmates.

"Then let's aim for the 25th. If we can get at least one person from each block on board before then, it could work," I trumpeted, hoping that the majority would back me up.

There was more silence as the plan birthed into a tangible living thing, with the countdown of just two weeks.

"You don't quite understand, Raya. Not every block would have a weapon, even if we have twenty-six at our disposal. The guards in the outer ring will have guns, not to mention the snipers. My crew can only take out ten to fifteen of the snipers, which will neutralize that threat, but the outer ring guards closest to the platform will be the issue," Marie warned.

"Most of us here witnessed the last execution, unfortunately, and most guards will be by the platform, like Marie said. It's to keep the rest of us at bay because emotions run high, especially depending on the victim," Shiri interjected to help me understand.

She bowed her head slightly in remembrance of Naomi's father. He was a well-respected member of our church, and no one could possibly say anything negative about him. He obviously didn't deserve the ending he received.

"That means blocks ABC and XYZ don't need weapons. They will have to overtake their one or two guards by sheer numbers, so we need most of those blocks on board, not just one for each block. The inner blocks...H through R...will be the key to our defense," Marie continued solemnly.

"I understand now, but I have another suggestion we should all consider. Y'all aren't gonna like it, but it's an option," I said with a look of unease on my face. "Me, Shiri, and Leah all work in the Laundry Center. I think I may have an idea of how to conceal the weapons in our uniforms. Don't we have a block that sews and patches up the damaged ones?"

"I thought I had taken care of that part when I convinced the Commander and Miss to give out the coats, but she must have sidestepped me and ordered the ones without pockets," Marie explained.

She then affirmed that block L worked in a sweatshop on-premise making undergarments for the corporate side of the Transcendent Program. They altered damaged uniforms for the inmates, as needed.

"Perfect," I announced. "Once we get the info for each brother and sister on board...H through R...we can tear holes in the sides for L to 'repair', but they actually sew a concealed pocket on the seam. It can be done easily with scrapes of discarded fabric. The pocket doesn't have to be large. Just big enough for the handgun."

"But that means the person has to take a demerit willingly," Leah argued.

"Yes, but then we will know who is actually down for the cause. If you are truly willing to sacrifice something, your fruits will bear record, right?" Mateo reasoned.

I could see a sudden epiphanic look pass across her face, and she raised her eyebrows and tilted her head slightly in complete agreement.

"That is a great idea, Raya. Let's get to work on this message system. It needs to be solidified," Marie exclaimed, clasping her hands together.

"We should start small, maybe get one or two blocks on board first. See how it works in application," Von ventured.

We all agreed before it was time to leave.

Marie suggested we involve D and R blocks first since they would be the leading message carriers with the food trays.

Shiri mentioned a sister she trusted.

"Bertha can get a message to her," Marie pledged. "Just tell her when you leave tonight."

Aaron, the otherwise quiet middle-aged man from R block, finally spoke up, "I can get at least four carriers on my block. I'll let you know how it goes next meeting."

Marie shooed everyone back to their barracks, telling us to meet in the boiler room again on Monday. We only had fourteen days until Liberation Day, and there was much to be done between that time.

Mateo passed a still-sleeping Rio to me, and I cradled her in my arms, feeling the warmth radiating from her tiny body. I bounced her gently to wake her up.

Once she fluttered her eyes open, I whispered to her that it was time to leave. She waved goodbye to her brothers and blew a kiss to them both.

"Good night, good night..." Mateo crooned lovingly to his baby sister.

She beamed and whispered in return, "...Construction site."

When we got into the vent, I asked Rio what that saying meant. She told me it was from her favorite book.

"Mateo wed it to me evewy night," Rio lisped.

I thought that Mateo definitely didn't seem like one to get himself caught up for an execution.

I hoped Von could live up to the occasion.

TWENTY-NINE

SOLO

10 PM. SUNDAY.

With Organic Truth music blasting through my earbuds, I bobbed my head and lip-synced the lyrics while welding the final piece of aluminum to the superconductor casing.

I was beyond ready to get out of this stuffy storage boulder. My neck had a crook in it from being unable to stand up all the way when I worked on the top of my EMP-like device.

I had to suspend the gadget with a wiring harness so it wouldn't touch and react with any of the storage building's metal or electrical sidings.

Yesterday, I chilled, read my Bible, and listened to my Fred & The Genius AHAYA playlist while the thing was suspended, open, and exposed over my head.

Bringing in the Sabbath alone, cramped in this quaint space, was strange, but it was more than necessary, so I endured.

According to Raya's recent transcripts, I had less than two weeks to implement my own plan to get to Mississippi by the 25th.

I applied the final caulking to the bottom crease of my machine, which looked more like an oversized steel school thermos. I laughed at it because it reminded me of a giant metal prescription pill. I could see myself rolling it to the TRP's front gate like a bowling ball and watching it quietly detonate.

This would be a game-changer.

But I also had to be careful with it.

After doing statistical testing, I learned that the device was unpredictable and volatile in its current state, so I couldn't take it back to the Sanctuary with me. It would have to stay suspended in this space until it was time to go.

I could have built a small Faraday cage for it, but I didn't have the materials here, which frustrated me immensely. I should have planned for this, but I was too anxious to leave and finish this part.

I would have to do it first thing in the morning.

In my mind, I pictured the Faraday cage fashioned in the shape of an old-school lunch box.

Ha! I'll make a Scooby-Doo lunch box lookalike with the whole crew standing before the iconic van.

I wondered how Juda was doing as I packed up the rest of my spare parts and materials.

Adina was working with him on some simple physical therapy exercises to get him upright again, but who knew how long that would take.

He would be devastated knowing he couldn't go to Mississippi on our most daring rescue mission yet, but I would have to fill him and Elijah in on Raya's planned Liberation Day coup, all the same.

I turned off the flashlight feature to my night vision glasses, switching them back over to their regular purpose, clutched my backpack, and listened for any approaching soldiers.

I heard nothing nearby, so I cracked open the boulder slightly, careful not to rock the intricate webbing holding up the EMP pill. I pushed my backpack out noiselessly through the slim gap, then squeezed myself through it, holding my breath to make myself thinner.

Even though it was below forty degrees outside, I was sweating nervously, trying not to widen the crack more than necessary, accidentally shaking the frail device I just spent days meticulously building.

I was glad no one was there to see me shimmying from under the storage boulder like a moron. It took me more than ten whole minutes to get the bulk of my body through.

Once I was finally free of the opening, I let the side go gently, making sure the keypad triggered the closure.

I could see my warm breath reacting against the frigid air through the thermal readers in my glasses, reminding me that we were well into a southern winter.

I shivered after the wind made contact with my sweat-soaked hoodie. I booked it through the woods, still nervous about the patrols. I hypothesized that the Syndicate soldiers must not have been very militant or obedient to their duties because it seemed like they were staying closer to the warmth of the house versus doing much policing out here.

Fine by me.

I made quick work of maneuvering back to the now barren Franklin tree with its rigid grey and white bark. I could still tell it was our marker tree because it had that single white flower lever attached to it. It was humorously out of place and seemed too obvious, so I pulled the fake flower off and stuffed it in my pocket. I would put it back in spring, Most High willing.

I pulled the now perfectly camouflaged lever and gained access to the tunnel. After opening the hatch, I removed my night glasses and climbed down the piped rungs, triggering the automatic overhead lights.

Noting that the door was secured, I breathed a husky sigh of relief to be back safe and sound.

Checking the time, I saw that it was not quite midnight. Maybe I could start work on the Faraday lunchbox. I really hated to pause in the middle of a project, and I felt like I wasn't done unless the box was completed for the small EMP.

My brain wouldn't let go of the thought and schematics of it. The shape and tools I would need to craft it pushed me into a conceptual loop, and the only thing that would alleviate my obsessive thoughts was to finish it all tonight.

Uncle Zeke's voice filled my head and countered my drive to complete the project. I could hear him lecturing me on getting my rest and starting again tomorrow.

Maybe just this once, I could let it go.

I walked the three miles in silence, mentally battling between the two choices before me...keep working...or go to bed.

My legs were on autopilot to my Lookout room, but they abruptly stopped at the Infirmary.

I decided to peek into the white, sterile room with only three med beds situated within. Only one bed was occupied at the far right end of the room, and to my astonishment, Juda was awake and sitting up, staring at the adjacent wall.

Someone had painted a picture of the Franklin tree in full bloom and framed it to the wall. He seemed fixated by it, even though the lights had been left dim.

I reached inside to find the control on the wall and turned the brightness up slightly. This act broke Juda's concentration, and he turned to face me.

"Hey," he acknowledged, his voice sounding more robust than before.

I returned the greeting and moved inside the room, looking for the chair.

He pointed to the corner where the supply closet was situated. The chair had been moved there, and I couldn't easily see it from the doorway.

"You want some company? What are you doing up?" I questioned.

"Solo, I've been asleep for over a month. I don't think it's gonna hurt me to be up a few extra hours now," he joked.

I smirked at his comment and relented, "Since you put it like that, I guess. Where did the painting come from?"

"I don't know. I was asleep, and when I got up a few hours ago, it was just there. It's really nice, though. It reminds me of Raya. Is that weird?" Juda added.

"Uh, naw naw. I can see that," I rationalized while squinting at the artwork. "Like she is the tree, right? Standing up to adversity alone."

Juda hoarsely laughed and ended up sputtering out a cough in the end before replying, "What are you talking about, man? No. You going too deep with it. I just mean, I remember when we planted them. Raya had come home going on and on about that dumb special kinda tree after a field trip, and Dad made us plant them so she would know how to find the Sanctuary. That tree was for her."

I bowed my head in remembrance.

I did recall that day.

Uncle Zeke had to special order them, and he bought way too many. Juda and I never did find out what became of the ones we didn't use.

"Adina told me that Ryan left," Juda continued, turning from me and focusing back on the painting.

"Yeah, he stayed by you for a week, fasting and praying, before he gave up and left," I accused, still feeling some type of way about him leaving like he did.

Juda looked at me again but in a serious pragmatic way, as if he knew something I couldn't possibly understand.

"He had to go...and I wish him well," he quietly reconciled.

I was baffled at his simple yet good-natured resolve. It was as if Juda had come to grips with Ryan's short term purpose and didn't hold any grudges against him any longer.

My face must have given away my thoughts and feelings because he flashed a half smile at me before replying, "Facing death will make you reconsider your ways, cuz."

I nodded in passive understanding.

"What's going on with you? Why are you roaming the halls like you just snuck back in the house?" Juda interrogated.

"I just got back from building my project. You know the one I told you about that will temporarily shut down all TRP power? There is one last thing I gotta build for it, but the supplies I need are here. I was headed to my Lookout to finish up," I rambled out, sounding guilty and caught, pointing in the direction of the Lookout.

"Um, okay. Did you hear anything else from Raya?" Juda asked, changing the subject, probably because I was coming off weird.

"Yeah, yeah, I did. She's planning an escape for November 25th. We have less than two weeks to get ourselves together, but I think everything will go smoothly. My team is ready, and the EMP is partially ready. We just need to figure out how to get to Mississippi without getting caught."

"Best way to go is the same way Raya went...get caught," Juda rationalized. "You know... but not really get caught."

I stroked my bare chin, deep in thought, then I laughingly murmured, "Seems everyone is smarter than me lately..."

I got up to leave because my body had betrayed my wishes. Now that I had sat down and rested briefly, it was a wrap. I wouldn't be finishing the Faraday container tonight.

I needed sleep in a real bed.

"We need more people on our team, if we are going to overtake a prison bus. I think they have one or two of them stored at the old house but we will need Syndicate soldiers to drive them as well. We are gonna have to kidnap somebody...or two," I said, validating Juda's suggestion, before exiting the Infirmary.

Juda let my words marinate briefly before revealing, "Then I'm going, too."

THIRTY

— ✦ —

RAYA

8 AM. MONDAY.

Thirteen days until Liberation Day.

I stood at the bars of my cell, alone, waiting to be released for work. I could hear Shiri complaining about her bunkmate snoring all night.

Shiri shared her space with an older woman who looked very much like the Crypt Keeper. Her skin was sagging loosely off her bones and joints and around her eyes. Her distinct sinus issue caused her to sniffle all night long when she wasn't actively snoring. I smiled faintly at the thought of Shiri staring death threats at the woman during the night while she lost precious sleep.

Once the automatic doors sounded and we were given reign to line up for work, a lady bumped into me ever so slightly and breathed, "We're with you."

I looked at her briefly, not recognizing her face, but she quickly moved away to her designated area before I could respond. I continued walking to my line, and again, another sister brushed against my arm and sighed, "I'm down. I'll take the demerit."

The word seemed to spread quickly in just two days, and volunteers were rallying to the cause.

I noted her prisoner number and repeated it to myself a few times rhythmically until it was solidly stored in my memory bank. I stopped by the far right wall, where the laundry line began, and stood ahead of Shiri, waiting for Marie to escort us like any other day.

Shiri leaned close to my back and whispered that we had two people on board from D, according to Bertha.

"I don't know who the second person is, but if Bertha trusts her, we should be fine," she murmured to the back of my head.

I nodded slightly and looked out broadly at all the other women in our block. In return, I received an abundance of approving looks in my direction.

Praise the Most High.

"This is gonna work. This is gonna work, Shiri. I can feel it. The Spirit is moving. This is actually gonna work," I asserted quietly.

"Of course, it's gonna work. Who said it wasn't gonna work? If the Most High is for us, who can be against us?" Shiri affirmed. "We just need to do our part. How are we supposed to find all these uniforms, by the way? Did you have a plan for that?"

I didn't.

I turned my head slightly so she could see my side profile.

"Ah...so we're just gonna dig until we find them, huh?" she questioned, perceiving from my side-eye glance.

I nodded in a self-critical manner, knowing that this was likely to be a significant hole in our plans. I started to wonder about Leah and how she was going to fare having to work by herself rummaging through dirty clothes, looking for needles in the proverbial haystack.

We would have to discuss this tonight at the meeting.

Marie finally showed up and walked us to the Laundry Center, and she was stoic as ever. She made no eye contact with any of us while she marched us to our workplace, still gripping the AR-15 for my sake.

Miss must not have released her yet from being my personal babysitter.

After she opened the door, H block inmates piled out from their shift, moving over to their right to let us walk by. Leah shot me a pleading glance from the H block line like she wanted to relay a message, but I didn't understand her facial expression because she always looked irritable.

All the fingers on her hands were twitching like she was mimicking washing hair.

Washing hair? What does that mean?

H block moved on, and we were pushed in, forced to take their place.

It was customary for me and Shiri to start at the overworked washing machines. Today, instead of doing a mad dash to get the clothes in, I carefully examined each uniform as I began stuffing them into the machine.

The far right machine sounded for more soap, so Shiri shifted towards it to oblige its request.

She whispered for me to come see, so I stuffed clothes into the middle machine and fluidly moved over to see what the fuss was about.

Clear as day, a prisoner's identification number was written into some spilled liquid soap on top of the machine.

"Well, that solves that problem," I said with a shrug and an inward laugh.

Shiri swiped at the detergent with her bare hand until nothing was left but a blurry blue mess.

I relayed to her the other number we had to look out for, and we both sang the numbers together in rhythm under our breath like a song only we knew the lyrics to.

My anxiety amped up with each hour that passed. Neither of us had located either uniform, and it was almost time for us to be dismissed.

This isn't going to work...this isn't going to work.

My thoughts were increasingly panicky, and even Shiri looked frazzled while handling the clothes. She spent an extra amount of time at the folding table, no doubt destroying her skin in heat blisters, just so that she could double-check all the uniforms we had already processed.

A few minutes before it was time to go, miraculously, there they were...both of them.

They were lying within the mountain of uniforms, waiting to be stuffed into the washing machine.

I bent down and said a prayer of gratitude, not even sure why I doubted in the first place. I took my longest jagged nail and popped a few threads in their seams under the right side armholes, then ripped down until the spaces were hand-sized. I was careful not to make the moves suddenly, noting the cameras in the corners.

I then walked them to the door and banged on it twice.

Marie opened the door and snatched the items, her facial expression never betraying her true character. After taking them, she slammed the door in my face. I knew she was playing her role, but that was just plain rude of Ryan's mom. I could hear the squeak of her army-issued boots walking the damaged uniforms down the long hallway to the sweatshop for repairs.

I returned to work at the clunky washing machines until Dark Shades banged on the door nearly fifteen minutes later, indicating that our shift was finally over and we could eat and relax for a moment before we had to 'wash the dishes with Bertha'.

After scarfing down the runny rice and gravy with toast, I drank half my water bottle and then looked for Rio.

"Have you seen Rio?" I asked Shiri, moving my neck from side to side, looking desperately down the long metal tables to no avail.

She shook her head as she searched, too.

It was time to discard our trays, so we got up and went over to Dark Shades guard post by the kitchenette.

Maybe Rio went to sleep early in her cell.

"We need to help Bertha wash the dishes," I announced mechanically, expecting to be let through immediately.

Dark Shades sneered at us and put her hand up to my shoulder in resistance.

"No dishes to wash today. Except for you. She can't come," Dark Shades snarled coldly.

She pushed my shoulder back slightly to let me know who was in charge.

I turned back to Shiri, and she quickly suggested that I go ahead.

"Tell me later," she petitioned, then walked away towards the yard without waiting for a response.

Dark Shades let me pass, and Bertha opened the darkened vent grate for me to enter.

I still hated this part the most.

I would always falter a little inside, and my thoughts would migrate immediately back to the Chute and the demonic chanting.

I held my breath longer each time I went into the vent, and I was almost up to two minutes this time. I couldn't justify why, but not breathing in the vent helped me focus on getting through.

As soon as I crawled into the utility room, I took long, deep breaths of the hot, acrid air. It reminded me of being in the laundry room but less humid.

Marie was standing in the middle of the room with her back to me, but when she heard me grunt and grumble my way out of the vent, she turned to greet me.

"Raya, thank you for coming. We need to talk...just me and you," she fretted, visibly looking nervous and down-spirited.

"Yeah, no problem, but what's going on? Why just me?" I asked apprehensively.

I wanted to trust Ryan's mom like I trusted him, but something still seemed off about her.

"Because many of the prisoners have heard about what you did to that guard, and believe it or not, it's riled a lot of folks up. They want to burn this place to the ground. And they are looking to back you if you decide to do it. The people are with you, Raya. Not me, or Mateo, or Von...or anyone else. It has to be you that encourages this," Marie explained.

Her words did not register well in my head. I literally was only trying to protect little Rio from that guard's brutality, not start a revolution.

I didn't know how to respond, so I said nothing and maintained eye contact, waiting for her to continue explaining.

"We can't meet anymore. Well, not until the day before liberation. We can't risk it. I think Miss Agatha knows something is up," she confided directly. "She is watching me watch you. It's weird. And she is making it hard for me to get time to myself. I have extra gate duties now when I'm not monitoring you. I had to make an excuse just to get this little bit of time now."

"I get that, but why still meet with me? What do you need me to do?" I asked snobbishly.

"Leah will give you whatever prisoner numbers she can't find. And be careful who you talk to about this. Just because someone may sorta know what's going on doesn't mean it's not a trap. Agatha is cunning and has moles all over the place. Don't trust anyone."

"I'm pretty good at discerning, and I didn't plan on talking to anyone else about this anyway. I get what you're saying, and I'll be careful. Everything will work out to the Most High's glory. I'm sure of it," I tried assuring her.

"I'm serious, Raya. I NEED you, in particular, to be careful. I've been here for six months, and I've seen some pretty messed up—"

I cut her off abruptly, asking, "Wait, what? You've been here six months?"

"—Yes, I've been here since April. Why?"

Ryan lied to me. He said his mother was taken to Mississippi in July. Why would he lie about that?

"No reason. I'm sorry for cutting you off," I pivoted swiftly.

"Okay...anyways, I've seen some pretty messed up things here. Miss is a certifiable lunatic...just like the Commander. Trust me, things are going on in this place that are worse than the Chute."

I stopped listening long before she finished her sentence. Her voice faded into the background of my own over-crowded thoughts.

Ryan said the Hebrew wedding was his first mission, and the Syndicate sent his mom to Mississippi the same day. He bold-faced lied to me.

"Did you hear me? Raya!" Marie all but shouted.

"Huh? Oh...yes. I will be careful. No worries," I dismissively responded.

She scrunched her face up in confusion.

"I asked you a question, though," she sighed, pinching her fingers between her brow.

"Oh, I'm sorry. I guess I didn't hear that last part," I responded, still in a daze.

She sighed heavily again, "Nevermind. Just be vigilant. You can go now."

She waved her arm in a frustrated dismissal, and I couldn't really refute it. I turned to go, and she watched me hesitantly descend back into the ventilation system.

As I made the first few shuffles down the vent, I heard her exit the main door, locking it securely behind her.

I felt terrible not paying full attention to her, but the Ryan math just wasn't mathing or maybe Marie was lying to me.

I already didn't trust her fully.

It was a real possibility.

My assumptions kept me occupied while I made my way through the dark metal vent.

When I came out the other side, I was at eye level with Bertha's thick legs, but a second set also lingered beside her. I looked up from my hands and knees position and recognized the complete profile of Naomi, standing there conversing with Bertha in a hushed tone.

Naomi looked down at me with a condescending smirk, "Hello, Raya...just the person I've been looking for. We need to talk..."

THIRTY-ONE

 ⬦

I STOOD UP AND brushed off the dusty patches of debris from the pants portion of my uniform. It plumed out of the fabric like thick chalk from a blackboard eraser, causing me to hack out a short cough.

Even still, I focused on this task with much dedication, patting the entire length of my uniform and pretending I wasn't doing anything out of the ordinary, just to avoid eye contact with Naomi.

My goal was to remain as calm and collected in her presence as possible, but on the inside, my heart was pounding beneath my rib cage in trepidation.

I no longer considered Naomi a friend after she callously attacked me in the hallway, but I wasn't sure what title she deserved from me now.

Either way, she had just caught me red-handedly crawling out of the vent shaft and was undoubtedly a Miss mole.

I feared the whole plan was now in jeopardy because of her unwelcome appearance.

Bertha seemed to pick up on my fretfulness and tried to ease my fidgeting by reassuring me Naomi's presence was sanctioned by her.

"Don't worry, chile, she alright. You can trust her. This my little messenger bird," she proclaimed while smiling appreciatively at Naomi.

Naomi returned a cold, disingenuous smirk to Bertha as she spoke.

This was definitely not the same person who went on rescue missions with me back at the Sanctuary.

Or was it?

Naomi was standing adjacent to Bertha and was gripping a greasy-looking stainless steel service cart, which was stacked full of barely clean food trays.

I glanced behind Bertha to the long, steel gray work table with its deep tub sink attached. There were very little supplies to use for cleaning.

Sitting by the faucet was a bar of hand soap, still sudsy from recent use. It had food bits ingrained into it.

I wondered how Bertha washed all those trays with that tiny bar of complimentary hotel soap and tattered dish towel.

I felt terrible that I had never actually stayed to help her wash the dishes, making a mental note to come back tomorrow if there would be a tomorrow for me.

That depended entirely on my conversation with Naomi and what she chose to do with it afterward.

"I'm listening," I answered cautiously, folding my arms together. I stood there in a defensive stance, ready this time if she decided to get froggy.

Naomi never let go of her grip on the service cart, pushing it slightly back and forth like a pram before she appealed, "Raya, I'm really sorry about the other day in the hall. You just don't understand. She punishes me when things aren't just right, and when the cake hit the floor, I just...blacked out. I didn't even realize it was you until that crazy guard hit me."

Naomi spontaneously reached for her left ear, still inflamed in pain.

I almost had a mimicking impulse to reach for my right eye, remembering the lick Marie got in on me as well.

Naomi hastily continued without pausing to breathe, "I don't know what her fascination with me is, but it's incredibly terrifying. She treats me like an equal one minute, and the next...you have no idea. I've been tortured, put in the Chute twice already, and she still won't leave me alone.

I've got to get out of this place, or she is gonna end up killing me when she finds some new pet to fixate on."

Naomi was getting tensely worked up, crazed in her statements.

"You have to believe me, Raya! I'm doing everything I can to help your cause. I just wanna go home!" she cried out too loudly.

My desire to comfort a distressed friend overtook my better judgment, and I let go of my rigid stance and stepped towards her to give her a reassuring hug, but she hissed out, "Don't touch me! Don't touch me!"

She maneuvered the cart between us quickly, using it as a shield from any human contact I might have tried to offer.

"Hush, chile! People will hear you," Bertha seethed in a muted voice.

Naomi seemed to suddenly remember her surroundings and breathed deeply and slowly before continuing in a more controlled tone.

"I can't keep living like this. I wanna help, and I am helping regardless of whether you believe me. I'll tell you everything I find out...like did you know Miss suspects a riot or something major coming? The next weapons shipment will be doubled, including tear gas and masks. She keeps ranting on and on about how ungrateful our people are when all she does is try to get us back to being true patriots to the country. That lady is crazy."

I felt very sorry for Naomi as she explained the reasons behind all her odd behaviors and maybe she truly deserved a second chance.

She looked deeply into my eyes and asked, "Do you forgive me?"

Dad's words vividly rang out in my mind:

> *One of the worst feelings we can experience in life is that after being good to someone, they reciprocate the opposite sentiments for your love. And one of the worst things we can do in life is to be that person. The Word of God is very clear;* **"Be not deceived; God is not mocked: for whatsoever a man soweth, that shall he also reap." (Gal. 6: 7)**

> *If you've experienced this kind of pain and disappointment, be encouraged to continue in well doing. God is faithful, and He will reward your good deeds. If you have caused others to feel this type of pain, be warned and repent!*

As believers, we are commanded to "do good unto all men" (Gal. 6:10). "Do unto others as you would have them do unto you" (Matt. 7:12) should also come to mind here, but some people misinterpret this passage of Scripture saying, 'do unto others as they have done unto you'.

Yet others disregard this saying altogether and choose to do evil unto those who have done them good, but here is the danger: PROVERBS 17: 13 Whoso rewardeth evil for good, evil shall not depart from his house.

Now, that's a frightening thought, seeing that we have all been guilty of this egregious error at some point or another.

However, there is a remedy!

The one way to overcome the evil recompense is to repent: **PSALM 37: 27** *Depart from evil, and do good; and dwell for evermore.*

And to those of us who suffer at the hands of unrepentant evildoers, be ever patient and continue to wait on the Lord. He will judge: **2 Thessalonians 1: 6** *Seeing it is a righteous thing with God to recompense tribulation to them that trouble you;*

"Yes, I forgive you," I vowed, with all of our history and memories swirling through my head. "We have to stick together, no matter what."

She nodded with tears brimming her eyes but made no move to come near me. She only swiped at her face to clear the emotion from it, then relayed that she had to leave but, again, would do everything she could to help.

I felt good about our reconciliation and praised the Father for allowing it. I would trust Naomi to do what she said.

I wished Bertha a good night after Naomi left and walked to my cell, still wondering where Rio was.

When I passed her open cell, she wasn't there, and I was getting anxious again.

Shiri stood in her cell by the bars, waiting for me to pass, while her cellmate tucked herself comfortably inside her coat and blanket for the night.

Once I neared her, she whispered, "Well?'

"She just said be careful. We can rewash the dishes next Saturday. Have you seen Rio yet?"

Shiri shook her head.

"I'm getting worried. Do you think she's in the Chute?" I choked out, not wanting to think the worst, but it was the only other possibility.

"I don't know," Shiri answered honestly. "Just try to get some sleep. Maybe ask Marie tomorrow."

I slumped inside my tiny cell and plopped down onto the hard bottom bunk.

How am I supposed to sleep with Rio missing?

Thirty-Two

──── ◈ ────

Solo

1 PM. Thursday.

Nine days until TRP Mission Trip.

"Here, let me help you."

I could hear Adina fussing over Juda down the corridor in the Infirmary all the way from my Lookout.

She barely left his side nowadays.

Juda had tried standing up by himself a few days ago when no one was around, resulting in him feebly falling out of bed. In pain, he was stuck on the ground for over an hour. He had refused to bother anyone by calling out for help.

Since then, she made it her mission never to let him hit the floor again.

She acted as his human crutch, resting most of his body weight on her while he muscled through her physical therapy exercises. He had lost a shocking amount of weight during his coma, and his legs now operated like stiff, un-giving toothpicks.

Thankfully, he made slow progress in gaining some of the weight back through a ravenous appetite. His flexibility, though, was still nonexistent. It was like teaching a baby to toddle; he mostly had to lean against something or someone to make progress anywhere.

Adina never let him skip his Willow bark tea regiment, either. She reminded me of a mother hen, and it was much the same as when she helicopter-momed her little sister, Zara.

Now, the child ran from her if she tried fixing her clothes, making a fuss about her meal portions, or whatever else Adina noticed that needed adjustment.

Juda had become a replacement dependent for her.

My thoughts returned inward, and I remembered what I had come in here to do.

A few tweaks were needed on the Faraday lunchbox design so I could test it again.

Looking down at the metal box before me, it didn't look like anything special, but I knew if I didn't get the dimensions just right, the EMP would be unstable on the route to Mississippi.

It couldn't roll or be jolted in any way while being transported.

If it accidentally went off on the bus, the engine would instantly die, as would all the cars within a five-mile radius. That would cause a lot of unnecessary carnage and pileups, which I wasn't ready to be accountable for.

I listened for the 3D printer to complete its latest workup on the foam mold that would be the basis of the cage's interior. After the mold was complete, I planned to melt down the scrap aluminum lying around my workshop into a mini mesh hammock of sorts.

I was pretty sure my calculations were precise, but I started to rework them on my largest touchscreen monitor just in case. I only had one shot to get the pour exactly right, and it had to be perfect, with no gaps or breaks.

I didn't have any more useable metal materials for a second chance.

Pulling out the mini stylus tucked behind my right ear, I set to work on the schematics and dimensions for the fifth time.

Everything had to add up.

Deep into my projections, my concentration glitched when coarse rapping sounded against the locked accordion door. I tried to ignore the sound, but whoever it was wouldn't leave and did not announce themselves so I could screen whether I wanted to engage with them or not.

Sighing aggressively, I tore my attention away from the monitor, walked over, and unlocked the door. After jerking it open in annoyance, I was faced with Juda, being held up partially by Adina.

"What's up, Solo?" beamed Juda, proud of himself for hobbling further down the tunnel than before.

My irritation immediately fell away at the sight of his accomplishment.

I smiled big and praised, "Look at you, man. Next thing you know, you're gonna be running circles around me again."

I moved away from the door to let them in.

Adina was careful not to force Juda forward, letting him take his time to get where he was trying to go, primarily by himself.

After gradually shuffling to a chair, he gripped it with both hands and directed his body around to have a seat. He had the finesse of an elderly man trapped in a nineteen-year-old's body.

"I wanted to catch up with you, cuz, about the road trip. I think you should make me some comms like you did Raya...but not no moles or anything like that. That's weird. Something else...I don't know. You'll figure it out," Juda said after making himself comfortable in the chair.

"You aren't going, Juda. Man, we talked about this. You can't leave. Not like that," I objected, motioning my hands up and down towards him, indicating the totality of his condition.

He frowned up immediately in a challenge, then quickly let his defense down.

His facial expression softened.

"We got nine or ten days until the plan is put in motion, and I'll be running those circles around you by then. Even if I'm not, I'm going, Solo," Juda decreed in a good-humored way.

He leaned forward and picked up my small Faraday prototype, flipping it carefully trying to figure out what it was.

"New lunchbox design?" he eventually asked.

"No, and put it down. That's the EMP carrier," I explained, turning back towards the calculations on the monitor and tapping the stylus against my chin in contemplation.

Adina was still standing next to him when he quietly looked up at her and asked, "Do you know what he's talking about?"

"Not a clue," I heard her loudly whisper back, her voice foreshadowed in laughter.

I looked at them again briefly and harped, "Don't worry about what it is. You aren't going."

Big Man leaned stealthily against the doorway outside and asked, "Where we going? Or not going?"

I sighed again.

It seemed like nobody wanted me to finish my projects.

In the past few days, I had been called on to repair wiring on a faulty grow lamp in the hydroponics room, patch a broken hose pipe attached to a washing machine in the laundry room, and unclog a duct in the ventilation system, all while trying to complete this stupid Faraday cage.

"We're going to Mississippi," Juda bantered.

He locked eyes with me when he said it.

I threw my head back and groaned, "Can I please just finish this? We only have a few days to prepare everything, and I'm sick of making mistakes."

"Everything happens for a reason, Solo. The Most High will get the glory from what is to come. Don't stress. Just pray. Be vigilante," Big Man advised solemnly.

I nodded my head but still felt overstimulated by all the company when I was trying to work.

"Hey everybody. We having a party up in here? And no one invited me?" I could hear Sheba awkwardly asking while walking up to the entryway.

"Yep. Come on in," Juda replied playfully, knowing I was becoming overwhelmed.

She stepped past Big Man, who was still at the door, and found another empty chair.

"Oh, Solo, before I forget...John said he is suspending the trust exercises until further notice. Not sure why, but—" she trailed off sheepishly and shrugged her shoulders.

"We have a special mission coming up, that's why. Very secret stuff. What was your name again?" Juda explained jovially while facing Sheba.

He seemed to have reverted to the version of himself pre-Sanctuary, constantly joking and smiling at everyone as if he had no care in the world.

Sheba gave him a bewildered look at the casual mention of a top-secret mission.

"Uh, I'm Sheba. What mission? There's no missions right now."

Juda leaned closer to where she sat as if he was about to reveal a great secret.

Then he shifted his eyes left to right suspiciously before explaining in a not-so-quiet undertone, "In nine days, we are gonna steal a few buses, kidnap some Syndicate soldiers, and take a road trip to Mississippi to break my little sister outta jail, but shhh. Keep that to yourself, okay? Don't wanna cause a panic."

Sheba's eyes grew in sizable surprise before she turned them on me.

"Why didn't you tell me it was in NINE days?!" she barked out like a slighted wife.

I rolled my eyes towards the ground, hoping she didn't catch me griping to myself.

"You knew about this. We talked about it. I just didn't think how soon it was happening was something to tell," I said, shrugging dismissively.

"But I wanna go. I am going. I'm going," she deliberated weirdly out loud.

"And if Juda is going, then I'm going, too," Adina meekly threw out. "Someone needs to make sure he takes his medicinal tea every day. We can't risk a relapse."

"Absolutely," interjected Big Man while Sheba made some audible noises of agreement.

"Oh my gosh! The whole world can go. I don't even care! Just...please...everybody...can y'all get out?! I have way too much work to do, and this isn't helping!" I exploded loudly.

All eyes were on me for a painfully long period of time as I huffed and puffed afterward.

Then Juda spoke up, "Okay. I think it's time for my nap. Nurse?"

Adina giggled at his reference and bent down to wrap his outstretched arm across her shoulders. They hobbled out slowly while Big Man and Sheba looked on.

"See ya later, son," Big Man offered.

Sheba gave me a nice nasty look and dismissed herself as well, closing the door behind her a little bit too roughly.

I crossed the room and locked the door.

Finally...

I had forgotten what I was doing, so I plopped down in my swivel chair and rubbed my temples to regain momentum.

The Faraday box lay upside down on its opening, and my calculations would have to be erased entirely so I could start from an unbroken chain of thought.

I had no desire to finish this project anymore. Well, at least not today.

Admitting defeat against all the distractions, I turned to the large monitor in front of me.

Reaching behind its dusty stand, I felt for the tiny box that only I knew was hidden there.

When I finally grasped it, I pulled it out towards the light to examine its contents again.

I shifted open the small matchbox-looking container and, with the stylus still in my hand, poked at the two-way transmitter that resembled a short, curly hair follicle.

The comm would be Juda's when we left for Mississip-pi.

THIRTY-THREE

— ◦ —

RAYA

4 PM. SATURDAY.

Night before Liberation Day.

Shiri sat across from me, nervously eating her slop and gulping down her entire bottle of water.

"Whoa. You aren't saving any for tomorrow?" I asked her, surprised because she was always so meticulous about conserving for the next day.

"No point. I'll be drinking all the water I want tomorrow," she slickly replied, her lips curling in a ridiculous smile.

Then she asked abruptly, "We're supposed to 'wash the dishes tonight', right?"

I nodded reassuringly, but there was a permanent sick feeling in the pit of my stomach ever since I met with Naomi.

Neither of us had seen or heard from Rio in almost two weeks, and when I stealthily questioned Marie in the halls about it, she remained tight-lipped even though I knew she had to have some information about her whereabouts.

My thoughts jumped back to our conversation about hope and distractions from it.

It wasn't sitting well with me anymore.

I just needed to know whether something terrible had happened to the child and, if so, who to recompense.

Liberation Day was tomorrow, and there would be chaos, but my primary mission would be to find Rio once it began.

I prayed she was not in the Chute or worse.

After finishing the meal I didn't want to eat, I wiped my mouth with the back of my coat sleeve, which was starting to turn black from overuse as a napkin, and placed my food tray with Bertha.

For the past week, each day after dinner, I took that tiny bar of soap and the overused dish towel and helped her actually wash the trays. She spent her time brushing runny food bits off them into the garbage, just outside the doorway, with her bare hands.

She did this before handing them over to me for rinsing and washing and we held light conversation during our time together. It turned into a welcomed routine.

Like free therapy.

Today, after setting the tray down onto the narrow slit of a window between the back of the kitchenette and the open dining area, I looked to Dark Shades and formally announced that Shiri and I needed to help Bertha 'wash the dishes'.

I couldn't see her cloudy green eyes through the sunglasses, but I didn't pick up on any resistance in her mannerisms this time, so we moved past her, brushing up against her shoulder since she had refused to yield by stepping aside.

She and Marie always took their guard charade way too seriously.

I greeted Bertha, and she replied with a warm, affectionate smile. I had come to respect and care for her as much as I did for Ms. Lynn back at the Sanctuary, although their personalities were notably dissimilar.

She allowed us entry into the constrictive vent, and we emerged out on the other side, anxious for this last meeting with the group.

Even though Shiri and I had done our part by ripping various-sized holes into the seams of over twenty uniforms, we had yet to learn how the rest of the plan had come along.

We didn't know if we were given the correct identification numbers or if we were dishing out demerits to unsuspecting people. There had been no updates from Marie since I last met with her almost two weeks ago.

The plan could have crumbled into nothing more than a fantasy for all we knew.

I was borderline desperate for an update.

Was all this for nothing?

The first person that came into focus after exiting the vent was Mateo. It would have been a much-welcomed face, but my first consideration was breaking the news about his missing sister.

He saw us crawling out and sprinted over to enquire, "Hey, Raya. Shiri. Where's Rio?"

All the built-up mettle and courage I had to break the news to him dissipated with the wistful expression on his face as he approached.

"Oh, uh...I don't know. She's probably resting. You know, big day tomorrow," I rattled off, too squeamish and uneasy to tell the truth.

"Oh," he replied, discouraged.

He gave a polite smile, then excused himself to walk back towards his brother to give him the update.

Shiri waited for him to retreat far enough out of earshot before reprimanding me with a backhanded slap to my arm.

"Why didn't you tell him the truth?" Shiri nagged with a disapprovingly dirty look on her face.

I rubbed the spot she attacked and stuttered, "I don't know. I just...froze. Did you see his face? He looked heartbroken. I couldn't do it. I just... I couldn't."

"That's still no excuse. He deserves to know. I'm gonna tell him—"

Shiri started stomping towards Mateo and Von, but I swiftly caught her left arm and begged, "Please! Just leave it be. They don't need the distraction from what they have to do tomorrow and I plan on finding Rio as soon as the commotion begins. It'll be fine. Just leave them out of it for now. Please."

She hesitated but still looked resolved to telling them the truth.

I maintained eye contact with her, my expression sternly petitioning for her silence.

She let out an exasperated gasp and relented, "Okay, fine. But this is on you."

I nodded pathetically before my gaze shifted and floated about the room.

Only ten people were here.

That didn't seem right to me.

We needed every body member for an update, so their absence was concerning.

Marie was talking covertly to Von in a corner near a looming furnace. They appeared deep into a hushed conversation.

When it seemed she was satisfied with its conclusion, she immediately addressed the group as a whole.

"Peace and blessings to you all. Since the Sabbath has now concluded, we can begin. I'm sorry, wait a minute. Let me back up a second. Let's pray first, then we can begin," she receptively stated, seeing that we were all fretful.

She distributed the bandanas to the females, and then Von said a prayer for the Most High to be with us as we stepped into the unknown and to give us victory against adversity, if it was His will and pleasing in His sight to do so.

Amen.

"Thank you, Von," she said, acknowledging him directly before turning back to the group.

"—Everyone...please remain calm. Everything is going according to plan, and tomorrow will be...Most High willing...Liberation Day. Everybody involved knows their position. We cannot fail. Von, you have to make your escape right at noon. The weapons shipment will arrive at eleven o'clock, and everyone will be supplied with theirs by then."

Mateo interjected, "We have some people missing. Do they know what's going on? Is there something wrong?"

The rest of us nodded in unison, all wondering the same thing.

Marie looked irritated for a moment, then quickly regained her composure.

"Everything is fine. A few people are still in the Chute after taking their demerits. You must realize that for some, this wasn't their first...or second, and they knew the consequences."

"Won't they be...unstable...after they get out? Would you still trust them with a gun?" Leah questioned in her cynical way.

Marie's brow creased, and her calmness began to fade away. I paid close attention to her now and noticed that her eyes were bloodshot as if she had been crying.

Her lip started to tremble, and her facade was cracking.

Within an instant, she buried her face in her hands and sobbed.

I was sure none of us had ever seen that amount of emotion coming from her or any of the other guards, for that matter, and honestly, it was frightening.

We waited in awkward silence while she blubbered and cried, unsure how to respond to the unexpected outburst.

Shiri finally dared to console her by stepping up and gently placing her arm around Marie's shoulder in a half hug. Marie flinched away, but Shiri didn't let up.

She pulled her into a full hug and gripped her tightly.

Mateo got up, then Von, then Leah, until eventually, we were all standing in a sweaty, forced group hug while Marie released her pent-up tears.

"I'm sorry. I didn't mean to...I'm sorry," she apologized after we all moved away to give her space again.

She sniffled and aggressively swiped at her wet checks and running nose with the back of her hands.

She shook her head vigorously in an effort to fully compose herself as if she could shake her feelings away. Then she smoothed down her already tidy uniform while we looked on.

She cleared her throat, then spoke in a more controlled manner and repeated, "I'm sorry. It's just...I've kept some things from you, and it's time for me to explain."

We all glanced at each other, confused but still in anticipation of some new revelation from the defecting Syndicate soldier.

"We are missing people because they went to the Chute and never made it out," she went on.

"—The Chute can kill you. And I don't mean by 're-leasing' yourself. It can literally fry your brain if you are weak-willed, and the body will ultimately follow. I'm sorry...the others didn't make it."

"Is that what happened to my son?"

I cut my eyes to the speaker and recognized that it was the same man who had made the prayer request for his missing son the first time we joined the meeting.

His countenance darkened, and his expression aged with anguish.

Marie averted her eyes and did not respond, but that, in itself, was response enough.

Before the man could erupt in emotion, Mateo spoke up, "Jeremiah 29:11 says, 'For I know the thoughts that I think toward you, saith the Lord, thoughts of peace, and not of evil, to give you an expected end.' Your son's life and death were not in vain. None of our loved ones' lives were in vain. We all have a purpose within His plan, Shawn."

Von picked up where his brother left off and proclaimed, "Just like when our forefathers were taken into Babylonian captivity, the Most High told Jeremiah to encourage His people, letting them know He wouldn't abandon them there. Jeremiah 31:16, 17 says, 'Thus saith the Lord; Refrain thy voice from weeping, and thine eyes from tears: for thy work shall be rewarded, saith the Lord;

and they shall come again from the land of the enemy. And there is hope in thine end, saith the Lord, that thy children shall come again to their own border.' Please don't give up hope, and don't let your son's sacrifice become meaningless."

Their words ignited a flame in the older man.

His face appeared locked in an expression of unwavering faith, and he offered a few nods of agreement while the agony departed from him.

The interaction had the same effect on the rest of us as we stood there on one accord.

We were ready, and any angst among us melted away with finality.

Marie peered down at her watch and acknowledged that it was time to leave.

"Remember your positions. Our messengers will deliver the weapons to those who have volunteered, and everyone else, just play your part," she concluded.

Everyone moved confidently to their vents while Shiri and I approached Marie to return the bandanas.

"What are we supposed to do tomorrow?" I asked Marie since we were never instructed to do anything besides rip the holes in the volunteers' uniforms.

"You've done enough already. Because of you two and Leah, everything has been going to plan. Just focus on helping wherever the Spirit leads you," she resigned.

"But I can fight. I'm a good shot. I can help. And so can Shiri," I insisted, looking over to my best friend.

"Raya, I understand, but please, can you trust me for once? There are so many things you don't know about this place. If...God forbid...something goes wrong, I...need you to survive, okay? You can't do that if they find weapons on you. It would be best if you remained untouched by it. Set apart."

I was starting to think that this woman loved to speak in cryptic riddles curdled with mystery.

"What are you talking about, Marie? No more games," I said, folding my arms in irritation.

She threw back her head and loudly huffed, "Just...trust me. Please! You both need to leave. Say your prayers and be ready at noon."

"Fine..." I breathed, submitting to the unknown and dropping my arms in defeat.

Shiri and I left the room and slowly managed through the vent, with her leading the way.

I was overwhelmed with relief that this would be the last journey through the constrictive air ducts.

After we came out on the other side, Naomi was once again waiting, but this time impatiently.

Her flour-dusted fingers gripped the food cart the same as before, and I started to wonder why she would never let it go. It was like some security blanket or emotional support crutch.

When Shiri saw her standing there, she got up, brushed herself off, and then walked past her and Bertha without so much as a hello or goodbye.

She still didn't trust Naomi and had a bit of animosity toward Bertha for allowing her into the fold in the first place.

Naomi's almond-shaped eyes followed Shiri as she exited melodramatically through the service door, pushing it harder than necessary.

"What's her problem?" she asked after she turned her attention back to me.

"Nothing. She's fine. Just a little irritated today. We got a lot going on. What's up? You ready for tomorrow?" I responded, trying to get her to focus elsewhere.

Naomi didn't seem too convinced by my explanation, but she dropped it all the same.

"Yeah, I'm ready. You?"

I nodded and teased, "Doesn't really matter if I'm ready or not. I'm not 'allowed' to do anything. But I plan on finding Rio. You still have no idea what Miss did with her?"

A glimpse of deception and then pain flashed through Naomi's eyes.

"I don't know where she is," she snapped arrogantly. "And even if I did, I couldn't help you."

Naomi gripped the cart tighter and rocked it back and forth again.

"And why is that? I thought we had an understanding. If you know something, you need to tell me, Naomi. Is she okay?" I persisted.

"I...really don't know, okay? Miss isn't exactly my BFF. She doesn't confide in me. I'm more like a...servant...who just happens to be around when some important things are discussed. But she makes me leave as soon as she thinks I'm listening too hard," Naomi retorted.

She began to sound deranged as she explained herself, like she was retreating inside a dark place in her mind.

I knew that feeling and the spiraling that a simple memory could trigger, so I let it go for the moment.

"Did you bring any other news?" I asked, trying to change the subject.

"No. I just needed to know if everything was still on for tomorrow and if there was anything I could do in the meantime," she mechanically answered.

Her gaze had retreated far into the recesses of her own mind, and her pupils were dilated.

She reminded me of Ryan's facial contortion when we went into the vault for the first time. He looked possessed, and Naomi had that same aura about her.

"Are you okay, Naomi?"

I reached out to grip her arm...to ground her mind, but she came back to herself suddenly and jerked away before my hand could make contact.

"Don't touch me," she said through gritted teeth, but more reservedly than the last time.

She did not yell out like before.

I retracted my arm and stood there waiting for an explanation, but none came. I hoped after we left this godawful place, she would open up to someone.

Maybe Elijah or Ms. Lynn could counsel her back to sanity because, clearly, she was struggling to hold it all together.

Knowing Miss was capable of great wickedness, I wondered what she had inflicted on Naomi to drive her into this mental ditch.

"What happens if this doesn't work, Raya?" she asked all of a sudden.

I saw the terror flood through her mannerisms while she rocked the cart.

"It has to work. If it doesn't, a lot of people will die tomorrow. Why are you afraid? God is with us. He has protected us so far, right?" I said sharply in return.

She looked to the floor and whispered something inaudible, but I thought I heard, "Has He?"

"What was that? I didn't hear you," I called out.

"Nothing."

Naomi maneuvered her cart, pushing it partially through the doorway to crack the door open.

"I have to go. Miss is probably wondering where I am," she spat out, then marched through the opening and was gone before I could press her into repeating herself again.

Bertha, who had made herself more or less invisible during our exchange, unexpectedly spoke up, and her voice jolted me with surprise.

"Such a shame. That witch, Agatha, has done her in. It's one thing to be hated by that woman and a whole other when she is fixated with you. Better to be hated, I say."

Bertha leaned closer to me and whispered, "I hear she makes them sleep at the foot of her bed, chained to the cold hard floor, just in case she has a bad dream or something and wants to torture them in the middle of the night. Just to make herself feel like she got control again. She beat 'em for no reason at all, too, whenever and with whatever she can get her hands on if they ain't quick enough to get out the way. Least that's what I heard."

"Hopefully, that's just a fake rumor," I commented, wishing rather than believing.

It was probably worse than the rumors.

Miss was maniacal for no other reason except simply the enjoyment of convincing herself that she was better than the rest of us.

"Well, we better get on out of here. Everybody gonna need a good night's sleep for tomorrow. I plan on getting a few licks in on some of those rude guards, too. I got plenty trays," Bertha professed animatedly while swinging an imaginary one through the air.

We laughed, and both headed to our cells, but I doubted sleep would grace me with its presence tonight.

I couldn't stop thinking about Rio, where she might be, and what was in store for tomorrow.

I would check the Chute first, then Miss' quarters.

Tomorrow was Wash Day, then Liberation Day.

I smiled to myself as I lay in my dark, hard bunkbed alone.

Liberation Day...freedom.

Thirty-Four

⸺ ✦ ⸺

Solo

6 PM. Saturday.

Night of TRP Mission Trip.

"We really doing this, huh?" James asked as we stood in the vault, picking out weapons for our impending road trip.

He stuffed rifles and semi-automatic handguns into an oversized black duffle bag, then lifted and lowered it, gauging the weight against his muscles.

He would be responsible for carrying the weapons the three-plus miles back to the old house and wanted to ensure he had a tight grip on it.

"Yep," I responded, looking for the ammunition boxes for the .38 caliber pistol I just pulled down from the shelf.

"So the plan is just to snatch a few soldiers and make them drive us to Mississippi?" he quizzed, trying to wrap his head around the quest at hand.

"More or less," I shrugged, still searching for the right ammo.

After locating the boxes, I stuffed two of them into my own backpack and then zipped the bag up.

"Ready?" I asked in James' direction.

"...more or less," he mumbled in return.

He placed his duffle over his shoulders, letting the strap cross his body.

We stepped out of the vault, and waiting in the corridor was the rest of the team standing in a tight semi-circle.

Everyone was looking towards me like I had all the answers.

It was strange.

It was like I had temporarily taken Juda's place. I wondered if he felt that way, too.

I looked at each person, ready and willing to lay down their lives to get our people back. Their faces held blank expressions, but I knew there was anxiety to complete this mission.

I stared at them in awe when Big Man disrupted my admiration.

"Solo...come on, man."

"Oh, sorry. I was thinking. My bad. Uh, so, okay. The plan is to get two Synidate soldiers and two buses on the road within the next two hours. If we leave by eight-thirty, we'll make it to the coordinates in approx-imately—"

I looked down at my phablet and the electronic map showing.

"—six hours. That puts us in position around 2:30 AM. We cannot stop anywhere on the interstate. It's too dangerous. So take care of what you need to take care of now."

James immediately set the duffle bag down near Big Man's feet and walked towards the stairs, headed to-ward the bathroom.

As I watched the back of him disappear down the stairs, I continued to the rest of the group, "When we get to the entrance hatch, I'll deploy my drone to help guide us through the woods and hopefully find two lone soldiers to grab. We'll all need to take turns...mon-itoring...them during the trip. The last thing we need is for one of them to try something heroic."

Everyone nodded in silent agreement. With no one speaking up with opposing suggestions, the plan was decided.

James eventually returned and shouldered the duffle again, and we all headed down the entrance leg of the tunnel.

Big Man, James, and John walked at the head of the group, with Charles, Deshawn, Hector, and Sheba occupying the middle. I hung back with Juda and Adina.

Juda had made extraordinary progress in the past week, pushing himself beyond the limit of reason.

He no longer relied on Adina as a human crutch, but his movements were still stiff, and he had a long way to go in physical therapy. He managed well during the trek, not falling too far behind the rest of the crew.

Although he was determined to stand his ground and be a useful team member, I still had reservations about him going. The last time he left the Sanctuary, he almost died, and here he was, putting himself at risk again.

"It's not too late to hang back, Juda. No one will think any less of you," I quietly mentioned while he shambled ahead.

Adina was on his other side, pretending not to listen.

"I'm good, Solo. Really. The Most High gives us an expected end, right? I'm at peace with whatever He decides for me," he said through a lazy smile and a limping gait.

I couldn't argue against that, so I left it alone and prayed for the best.

Tucked under my right arm was my clunky, sky-blue drone.

Juda asked why I brought it again.

Since waking up, he forgot things and had to be reminded at times.

I patiently explained to him that I planned to use it to guide us safely to the stored prison buses using the night vision glasses as a Bluetooth monitor connected to it.

"Who's gonna guide you then?" Adina asked, finally letting down her facade that she was deaf.

Apparently, Sheba was also listening intently to our conversation because she turned slightly around and volunteered eagerly.

"This can be our trust mission," she giggled.

Oh boy.

It took us over an hour to make it to the entrance hatch, with everyone being mindful of Juda's condition, but the timing was still good.

I worked my way to the head of the group and went up the rungs first to disengage the lock. I entered my birthday into the keypad, the hatch clicked open, and I swiveled the lid for everyone to exit.

After checking to see that it was clear, everyone climbed out of the hole in the middle of the woods into the cold night air.

I immediately zipped up my coat while Big Man lifted Juda out, then secured the hatch.

I bent down to take off my backpack and unload my many electronic trinkets and treasures. I hastily pulled out the matchbox container and handed it to Juda.

"Okay? What's this?" he questioned, barely able to see in the moonlight.

"Here—" I said and turned on a small flashlight so he could see the contents of the container better.

"Okay, Solo...what am I looking at? This looks like a stray piece of hair. Ew, man. What is this?" Juda added, grossed out and trying to hand it back.

I smiled big.

"That's what it's supposed to look like. But it's not a piece of hair. It's your comms. You can put it near your hairline so no one will know you have it on. I upgraded it to an all-in-one. You don't need a receiver like Raya did," I said, too excitedly.

Juda still had his nose turned up at it but took it off the holographic backing and asked Adina to stick it on where it would camouflage with his hair best.

She put it on the left side of his face, just where his hairline dipped by his ear.

"Is it on?" Juda asked.

I looked down at my phablet and immediately saw his transcript coming in.

"Yeah. It's on."

Juda grinned in satisfaction that he got his request after all.

"Thanks, man," he simply said.

I went back to rummaging through my backpack and pulled out the night glasses and the controller for the drone. Soon, the propellers were lightly humming above us.

I explained to the group that we needed to stop at the storage boulder near the pond so I could collect the EMP.

"It's precarious, so once we get close, only I should go near it."

"Yeah, definitely sounds like you need to pre-carry whatever it is you're talking about," James thoughtfully responded.

Adina put the back of her hand up to her mouth to stifle a giggle, and John gave a gruff, irritated sigh at the boy.

Sheba stepped up to my side and placed her arm through mine as I started to navigate with the drone. She pulled me away from dry gulches and sharp rocks that would otherwise trip me as we went along.

"We have to head north, then veer west to get to the outcropping of storage boulders. There were soldiers camped out there the last time I came, so be on the lookout," I instructed quietly.

As a tight-knit unit, we continued swiftly through the woods, barely rustling the crunchy leaves. Everyone wore all black to blend effectively into the night.

Big Man, John, and James were outfitted with large hunting knives while Hector, Charles, and Deshawn toted half-raised rifles.

"There," I breathed.

I pushed the night vision glasses onto the top of my head and handed Sheba the controller. After giving her basic instructions on how to keep it neutrally in the air, I moved slowly toward the boulder's hidden keypad.

There were no soldiers nearby tonight, which I thought was strange. We hadn't run into any in the nearby vicinity either.

Taking my backpack off again, I reached in to get the lunchbox replica Faraday cage and opened it.

I carefully cracked open the storage boulder, slowly pushing it up to avoid disturbing the still-suspended EMP device. I shuffled underneath the opening until I could easily reach the device. Putting the Faraday cage under it, I took it from its suspension wires, laid it cautiously in the box, and closed it snugly inside.

I let out a breath I didn't realize I was holding, ecstatic that the hard part was over.

The EMP was stable inside the case because I had painstakingly ensured the construction was precise. The box could be dropped, kicked, or stomped, and the device would still remain secure.

I pulled myself out of the boulder and let it rest, re-engaging the closure. After stuffing the lunchbox replica back into my bag, I collected myself, realigned my glasses, and took control of the drone.

We stood momentarily while I maneuvered it a quarter mile out, closer to the house. I was picking up no thermal readings whatsoever.

Could this be a trap?

I glimpsed the shape of the two white prison buses parked on the dirt driveway near the tan-paneled house.

That house...our house, seemed eerily dark and quiet, but someone had to be nearby, or the buses wouldn't still be parked there.

Right?

I reasoned with myself that we should press on.

I felt nothing in my spirit holding me back.

"The house looks abandoned. But still, be careful. They could be hiding anywhere," I explained to the group.

Those with rifles stepped out of our formation and continued slightly west, ensuring we had cover.

Sheba linked her arm back in mine, but I dropped her grip by bringing my arm down to my side.

The drone came humming back, and I landed it on the ground nearby.

Switching the glasses from the drone's visual output back to my own, I stammered, "I got it from here, sis."

"No problem," she said coldly, trying to mask her troubled feelings.

I picked up on her indignation and tried to explain, "We don't need the drone anymore, and I need my...arms...to carry it."

She didn't respond to me and kept moving with the group.

After retrieving the drone, I ran to catch up, and we continued the quarter mile until the wood line broke, giving way to the grassy, sloped hill leading to the house and adjacent dirt road.

The light paneling of the house gleamed against the darkness and caused a floodgate of memories to pour forth.

I lifted my night vision glasses and glanced over at Juda and saw the same look of reminiscence on his face.

Just a few months ago, we would have been putting up lawn chairs and breaking down the enormous white tent we used for church service.

Uncle Ezekiel would have us stack everything in the shed, and then, depending on whose turn it was to decide, we would do some kind of family activity together.

Juda always picked movies. Raya mostly gravitated towards a trip out for ice cream.

I never cared.

I was just happy to be there.

"Let's split up," Big Man broadcasted, snapping me out of my daydream.

He, Charles, Deshawn, James, and Sheba collected themselves in an unspoken offshoot, leaving me, Juda, John, Hector, and Adina in the secondary group.

Hector and John led the way to the first bus, whose retractable door was strangely already open.

I pulled off my night vision glasses and took the small flashlight out of my pocket, shining it through the windows as we approached from the rear of it.

The seats on the dark bus were empty, and John went inside to look for keys while Hector and Juda stood guard outside the door. Adina stayed close to them, appearing ready to bolt at any moment.

Allowing the others ahead, I stuck a tiny tracking device under the bus chassis while they weren't paying attention. Then I went around the other side of the bus, outside their line of sight. I approached the front, attaching a circular camera near the wide windshield.

"I found the keys," John announced, pulling them down from the sun visor.

A loud commotion and a single gunshot drew our attention towards the house.

Big Man's small team came running towards us, dragging a man wearing the blue camo uniform. He was cursing at them loudly. James and Deshawn each tightly gripped one of his arms while hustling for the bus.

"Get on the bus! Get on the bus!" Big Man hollered over the soldier's ranting and waved to go, go, go.

A few seconds later, we saw three other soldiers emerge from the side of the house with weapons drawn. They fired on us, and everyone started to scramble onto the nearby bus.

Already inside with the keys, John started the vehicle. More shots rang out, and bullets struck near the driver's seat. He ducked but still held the steering wheel tightly.

Now occupied behind him in the front row of seats, I pulled out the pistol I had tucked into the waistband of my pants and returned fire through the shattered side window, giving Big Man's exposed team cover. John threw the bus into reverse, barreling backward towards the soldiers, but they were quick enough to escape the hit-and-run attempt narrowly.

I could hear Juda yelling from the steps of the bus through the open door for everyone to hurry up. Then he jumped out and refused to get back on when Adina started yelling at him to do so. He returned fire at the soldiers until Big Man's group reached the bus.

Juda struck two of the soldiers, causing them to retreat with non-fatal injuries, and the third took cover behind the shed off the side of the house. I could hear the last soldier loudly fumbling with a two-way radio, looking for a clear channel to call for backup.

With everyone safely on the bus, Juda haphazardly climbed up the steps so we could take off. I shook past him when he reached the top step, nearly knocking him down.

I had to stop that soldier from calling for help.

The whole mission depended on it.

We wouldn't make it far with an entire Syndicate army on our trail.

John looked agitated that he had to wait to pull off.

I exited by jumping past the last step, and before Juda could question me, I turned and blurted out, "Don't die," while shoving my backpack into his unsuspecting arms.

I took off full speed into the woods with the pistol aimed towards the shed.

I could hear Juda scream, "What are you doing, Solo?!" but John must have sensed that I didn't want them to wait for me.

I didn't have to turn around to confirm it.

I could hear the bus lurch in a sharp U-turn, heading away from the house towards the main road, while I sprinted at the soldier.

He was still fiddling with the radio dial, but as soon as he heard me rustling nearby, he dropped it out of fear. He raised his high-powered rifle shakily, but I was quicker.

I shot at his shoulder to disable him.

He moved the wrong way at the last minute, causing the bullet to strike him in the middle of his neck. Before his body hit the ground, I turned quietly back into the woods, disappearing into the night.

I headed toward the Franklin tree, running at full speed in pitch-black darkness. The route was so ingrained in my instincts that I could have made it back with my eyes closed.

Once I got there and pulled the lever to enter, I secured the hatch and continued sprinting the three miles to my Lookout.

Unlocking the door, I quickly pulled up all the security monitors and coded in the tracking device and camera I had planted on the white prison bus. Visuals popped up of the interstate they occupied, and the tracking beacon proudly confirmed their location.

I put my headset on, turning off Juda's transcripts and switching it to live audio.

"Juda, can you hear me?"

THIRTY-FIVE

— ◆ —

"I CAN HEAR YOU, Solo. What in the world was all that about?!" Juda barked out, still shocked that I wasn't on the bus with them.

"A soldier was trying to call for backup. I had to stop him," I struggled to respond.

All the sprinting left me breathless, and I bent over to collect myself.

"This was not the plan. None of this was part of the plan! We only have one bus, and we're driving blind!" he complained loudly.

I sat down exhausted in front of the monitors and tried to explain that I would get them there.

"How, Solo? Your drone is sitting right here on the front seat next to me," he retorted.

"Give me a sec...give me a sec. Need to. Catch my breath," I huffed.

The line got quiet for a moment, but I could hear the mechanical movements of the bus, driving full speed down the roadway.

"Okay...okay. I think I'm good now. I put a tracking device under the bus and a camera on the front. I can see what you see. Where is the soldier?"

Juda hesitated a second before replying that he was tied up in the back of the bus.

"Why isn't he driving? Wasn't that the whole point?" I questioned.

"Well, apparently, to get him to...comply...James shot him in the leg. He can't drive," Juda fumed, probably staring at James as he said it.

You got to be kidding me...

"Okay. Alright. That's not a problem—"

I hacked into the Georgia Department of Transportation and LexisNexis system to overtake their automatic plate readers all along the roadway. The cameras picked up car registrations every few miles, and I could see if any impending threats were approaching.

"Y'all are good. I hacked into GDOT. There aren't any police or unmarked cars nearby. I'll run the program the entire way. It will be fine. It's dark out. No one will be able to see John driving. Hopefully," I explained, trying to override his apprehensions.

I could hear John telling Juda he knew how to get them to Mississippi through Florida but wanted to confirm the route with me.

"Did you hear that, Solo?"

"Of course," I responded, pulling up the maps and giving him instructions on how to reach I-10, heading west.

With the headlights on, I could see the road as clearly, if not more precise than them, since it was a wide-angle camera.

After a few minutes of traveling, Juda moved towards the back of the bus where Big Man was interrogating the Syndicate soldier.

I could hear him asking why only four were at the house. The soldier refused to speak until I heard him cry out in pain.

"Okay! Okay...they relocated the base to Atlanta. Our Commander found who he was looking for...we were left behind in case any stragglers were caught," the soldier panted.

I wondered if he was talking about Raya.

"Ask him who they were looking for," I suggested to Juda.

He did, but the soldier would only repeat that he didn't know before he passed out in pain.

I heard Juda ask Adina to tend to the man's wound.

Then I heard him shuffling.

He must have been moving back to the front of the bus in his impaired way.

I picked up on the other team members conversing about what to expect once they got there.

Juda was silent, so I took the opportunity to explain to him what he would find in my backpack and how the EMP worked.

"So, let me get this straight...this thing will knock out all of their systems for thirty minutes only?" Juda surmised.

"Right. Oh, and before I forget, during those thirty minutes, you won't be able to communicate with me. You'll be on your own then. Find Raya and give her the small yellow box in my bag. It's a new receiver for her mole comms. Hopefully, the takeover will be complete once their systems come back up, and I can hack into them to reroute everything for you."

While Juda remained quiet, seeming to conserve his energy, I scoured the bus camera footage every few minutes for the first four hours of their trip, not seeing anything of interest.

Not much was being said on the bus in general as they traveled on. Maybe some of the crew was taking advantage of the time by sleeping.

They were still correctly heading west on I-10.

As they neared Mobile, Alabama, I spotted a broken down red Camero with smoke emitting from the engine compartment on the shoulder of the roadway about a mile ahead of them.

I ran the plates out of curiosity as something to do to keep me awake and alert.

The registered owner's name made my heart skip a beat.

"Juda! Tell John to pull over," I bleated out hysterically.

"What—" he sleepily responded.

"Pull over! Pull over! Now!"

Juda told John to pull over, to which John hesitantly complied.

It was 1 AM, and he knew they only had about an hour to go, so to pull over now must have confused the militant man.

I could see the bus stopping a few yards behind the incapacitated Camero. As the bus halted, a young white male emerged from the driver's side of the car and started to walk towards the bus.

"I don't know about this," I heard John allude.

My suspicions were confirmed as soon as he got closer to the front camera of the bus.

The door to the bus retracted open, and I could hear Juda call out to Ryan after he made his way down the steps.

"Can't drive an ATV...can't drive a car..." Juda laughed and dapped Ryan, giving him a half hug simultaneously.

In his deep baritone voice, Ryan chuckled nervously and replied, "You're alive!"

"Of course I am. And better than ever," Juda joked while he limped back onto the bus. "Come on, man. Looks like you need a ride. Lucky for you, we got plenty of space."

Ryan still sounded apprehensive in his reply and mentioned that he wasn't alone. He then whistled sharply, and two smaller bodies emerged from the backseat of the downed vehicle.

A brown-skinned teenage girl made an appearance, sporting six thick hanging plaits. She was holding the hand of a light-skinned younger boy who was clearly interracial.

"This is my sister, Dakota, and my brother, Logan," Ryan explained.

There were no follow-up questions, to my dismay.

It seemed like he and Ryan had some unspoken agreement between them to don't ask, don't tell.

I wanted to know how Ryan found his siblings and where they were headed when he broke down.

Ryan told his sister everything was alright; he knew them, and they could be trusted.

If she replied to him, I couldn't hear her muted response.

After they got on the bus, John closed the door pulley and merged back onto the interstate, determined to make it to Ocean Springs within the hour.

THIRTY-SIX

⸺ ✦ ⸺

RAYA

8 AM. SUNDAY.

Liberation Day.

I stood restlessly by the bars of my tiny cell, waiting to be let out so I could line up for the showers.

With the stench of the barracks tickling my nose, I couldn't wait to feel clean before gaining my freedom. This would be the opportunity to cleanse all our physical grime before wiping out our mental oppression.

It was surreal.

The day was starting like any other, but prayerfully, it would end in a spectacular uprising.

Today, we would go home.

Our electronic cell doors buzzed, and we were soon released to line up numerically. I found my place behind Shiri but mindlessly looked back to where Rio should have been. She loved wash day. But her tiny body wasn't present in the line. I turned back around, still on edge about her extended disappearance.

Dark Shades walked the line, ensuring we were all in proper order to head towards the showers. As she passed me, I heard her mumble, "Morning, Renegade."

Her lips turned up faintly as she said it, but she continued on with her inspection. I stared ahead of me, ignoring her jest as she passed.

I moved closer to Shiri and whispered, "Can you believe it? It's today. Today, Shiri."

She turned slightly and breathed, "I know, right."

The line started to move, and we were marched through the maze of back hallways until we reached the shower rooms, where I impatiently waited for our turn to enter.

The entire atmosphere was charged with rare anticipation while we stood there. Everyone felt the tide turning in our favor, even with just the rumor of impending change.

The ladies fidgeted in line, whispering to one another, and Dark Shades had to command our compliance to the rules several times. Although, she did it loosely, not bothering to dish out demerits to the caught transgressors, as was her duty.

After twenty minutes or so, Shiri and I took our place inside the washroom, grabbing the pitiful excuse for shower preparations provided. I took my provisions and located an empty, mildewed stall near the rear of the room.

After peeling off my week-old clothes, I situated the flimsy shower shoes onto my coarse feet and stepped into the tepidly heated water.

We were given roughly ten minutes to shower, so I quickly bathed myself and washed my cropped hair, scratching at my scalp to clear off the buildup of crude.

When Dark Shades banged her baton on the wall and bellowed that we had one minute remaining, I stepped out, wrapped in the gray, scratchy towel.

My freshly washed secondary uniform appeared on the bench, and I hurriedly put my clothes on. Even though the water wasn't freezing, they didn't exactly turn the heat on for us either. I shivered still after I had fully dressed and slipped the unwashed coat back on. The coat was already a dingier gray from constant use.

Miss probably would have had them discarded or burned once the season changed. Thinking back to the day of assembly, she had not bothered giving any instructions on having them cleaned.

As always, we were escorted to our work detail, but Marie was nowhere to be seen. Another female guard took her place by my side to babysit me with the AR-15.

I prayed silently that Marie was okay and her absence was just a part of the bigger plan at play.

I wasn't sure if I could handle waking up another day in this place just to commence the same spirit-breaking cycle of work, eat, walk, sleep.

Today had to be the day of liberation.

Admittedly, the new guard's presence did not sit well with my spirit because I couldn't tell if she was friend or foe. She could have easily been one of Marie's sleeper agents, but there was nothing discernable about her to tip my judgment one way or the other.

We were allowed into the laundry room, and everyone got to work lazily. It didn't seem much point to shoveling the clothes into the washers and running around drying and folding them afterward.

Shiri called it 'busy' work and kept at it to keep her mind glued to a distracting task. She was starting to look shaky and nervous as the time marched on.

"Don't worry, friend. Everything that is meant to be will be," I whispered to her while bending down for more uniforms.

As I said my comforting words, we heard a procession of army-issued boots walking purposefully toward the Laundry Center.

A loud, one-sided conversation occurred with the soldier guarding the door, and then we heard a sickly thud before the door violently swung open.

Miss angrily pointed at me and thundered, "Take her!"

Four Syndicate soldiers immediately descended on me, grabbing my arms and legs while zip-tying my hands together.

Amid the confusion, I didn't even have a chance to fight back.

Shiri screamed out for them to let me go, but she was quickly silenced by the aggressive backhand of Miss across her face. She immediately crumpled to the floor, and one of the other women bravely approached, pulling her far away from any further altercation.

I wailed out, asking what I had done.

Miss walked up to me and bent down to peer into my eyes devilishly as I struggled unsuccessfully against the soldiers' grip.

Her voice accusatory, she hissed, "What have you done? What. Have. You. Done..."

She straightened herself again and ordered the soldiers to take me to the yard.

"Wait, wait—" I begged, but to deaf ears.

The four soldiers picked me up by my arms and legs, carrying me out like a lamb on a spit.

As we passed through the doorway, I witnessed my new female guard unnaturally still on the ground.

She was folded into a pretzel in the corner. Another of Miss Agatha's guards now gripped her weapon while standing over her body.

I began to analyze everything around me as I tried desperately to set myself free. I hopelessly searched for indications of why I was being hauled away like an animal sacrifice.

Then I saw her.

Cowering with her cart and standing at the beginning of another hallway, Naomi gave me a bizarrely curled downward smirk that dripped with trickery as I passed.

My chest caved in with instant understanding.

To my disbelief, Naomi was not only a mole...she was a rat.

I could hear Miss traipsing behind me and my unrequested entourage. She called out murderously to Dark Shades before we reached the yard, "Call an assembly. NOW! We are going to have ourselves a good old-fashioned public execution today."

Dark Shades took off down another hall at her command.

The temperature plummeted as soon as we stepped outside. I could feel the frosty bite of winter rush through my uniform and thin coat.

It was an unexpected environment shift from the hot, sticky laundry room, but I welcomed it against my skin as my blood started to boil in anger toward Naomi.

She had betrayed me when I had forgiven her.

The guards dumped me on the ground while a second set of soldiers brought Miss' portable platform into the middle of M block's section of the yard.

Miss bent down, and just before she reached the proper distance needed for me to headbutt her in the face effectively, she warned, "Don't try anything funny, Raya, or I will squeeze the life out of your little babydoll right in front of you."

"Rio's alive?" I questioned in relief, then quickly regained myself.

"Prove it!" I spat out at her.

She laughed maniacally before replying, "This isn't some superhero film, Raya. Just be satisfied knowing that if you cooperate, she will be spared from witnessing your death. Otherwise, she can go first—your call. Makes no difference to me...you've already ruined most of my little social experiment anyway. I'll have to start over with someone better."

I looked at her, horrified and confused. Nothing she ever said made sense.

She saw my face contort in ignorance and lamented, "I swear. You people are about as dumb as a bag of bricks. All of this—"

She looked out at the buildings and waved her arms around her to indicate the entire compound.

"All of this is bigger than you. This country was founded upon principles that made no room for your kind. The only purpose you serve is for the greater good of our economy. Corporations, GDP...no? You're not getting it?"

I stared at her angrily but said nothing in reply.

Miss closed the space between us, challenging me with her hateful eyes.

"You think you're tough, Raya?" Miss snarled in my face.

I almost gagged from the smell of rank coffee permeating from her lips.

"We're about to see how tough you really are. They'll all see! I will break their spirits by freeing yours...though you don't deserve it."

Miss stepped back slightly and yelled unnecessarily into the wind, "Get her up! Put her on the stage."

The nearest soldier ran up and snatched me from the ground. Another came to assist him, and together, they hauled me toward the stage as I refused them the use of my legs.

After dragging my dead weight onto the barely raised platform, I was again slammed down. The resulting pain was starting to radiate down my right side.

Miss casually moved my way again but did not attempt to ascend the stage herself.

The two guards stood obediently next to me while we waited for the people to assemble.

Rows of inmates were starting to trickle out into the bitter cold.

Miss apparently couldn't keep herself from talking while we waited because she continued to scold me, "Raya, I had big plans for you. You have no idea. Your father didn't have the same potential as I see in you. You could have set a perfect precedent for your people...IF you had just stuck to the Program."

She started to pace slightly to warm herself, becoming increasingly agitated as we waited.

"I wanted to take my time with you. We moved too fast with your father, but YOU...oh, you! I knew from the moment you stepped foot in front of me...your transformation could have been one for the history books!"

She kept insinuating that my father had been here, but how was that even possible? I watched in horror as my mother languished over his lifeless body, lying there in the bloodied grass.

"Is he...still—" I coughed out before she interrupted in a fit of hysterical laughter.

"You don't get to ask questions, Raya. You don't get to know!"

This woman is stark, raving mad.

She abruptly stopped laughing, smoothed down her blue camo uniform, and said more seriously, "Well. No matter. You can still serve a greater purpose as an example to the rest of these ungratefully blind bats."

She stepped onto the stage and shooed the guards away.

"On your knees, please," Miss commanded politely.

I wiggled myself into compliance and stared down at the gray-washed wooden planks holding the stage together, tracing the wide cracks that hinted at a dry, dusty world beneath.

It was all I could do to remain tethered to serenity.

All our plans...just for my life to end here...like this.

I reasoned with myself that it would still be Liberation Day, but only for me. I had clear aspirations in the Lord for eternal life after this fleshly one ended.

I accepted my fate, and I wasn't afraid.

More people flooded out into the yard to witness the execution.

I peered out briefly and saw confusion and anger on many of their faces. The assembly wasn't supposed to happen until noon, and the wrong person was onstage.

I randomly caught Leah's eye as she stood before H block's inmates. I could never accurately read her, but she looked provoked and irate.

She raised her chin at me, then disappeared behind a few other women.

I turned my attention back to the planks and waited.

Once Miss was satisfied that every soul was present, she began, "What an unfortunate day we have upon us. It seems plans were made to defy the Program, which is absolutely not an option for any of you. Your ringleader, I'm told, wanted to lead you astray...lead you to hope."

She paused and firmly looked out to the crowd, eyes scanning each block of inmates.

"—But hope is a dangerous thing. Witness where hope REALLY leads," she crowed at full volume, pulling out a G43 pistol from her hip holster, then pointed it at my head.

I closed my eyes in anticipation.

The loud clap of a single clip punctured the air.

Then, complete silence.

Am I still...here?

My eyes peeled open ever so slightly as Miss searched for the source of the sound. The gun in her left hand was still pointed at my head. She gripped her right leg as crimson started to stain her uniform.

A ground-shaking crash resonated from the direction of the gate, then the clamoring sound of bullets followed, accompanied by muffled screams.

I had an overwhelming inner call to action in the space of Miss Agatha's hesitation.

While on my knees, my right leg shot out under Miss' legs, sweeping her forward. She lost her footing, causing her to fall promptly from the stage. She made a guttural noise as she descended before the crowd, losing her weapon.

As soon as she disappeared from my line of sight, I heard Marie's distinct voice yell, "NOW!"

Shots rang out from the guard towers and into the crowd. Soldiers started dropping like flies all at once. It happened so quickly that all the frantic motion over-stimulated me.

I remained parallel to the platform's planks, covering my head with outstretched, zip-tied hands. I foolheart-edly imagined that I was protecting myself from stray bullets.

Miss' gun lay on the stage a few feet away, taunting me. I wanted to use it for cover...to go find Rio, but all the bullets whizzing by paralyzed me.

"Help!" I screamed into the chaos. "Somebody help me!"

But no one heard or paid attention.

I looked into the crowd and watched the fight unravel before me. People were fist-fighting and shooting. There was a blurring of blue uniforms with gray and a sprinkling of people dressed in all black.

When I pulled on all my willpower to focus on those that were out of place, Naomi materialized, blocking me from making sense of what I saw.

She held a pair of small silver scissors in her hands, and without giving me time to decide my reaction to her presence, she cut the zip ties off my wrists and forcefully pulled me down from the stage. I fell hard on my stomach, momentarily knocking the wind out of my lungs.

Miss' weapon was still within arm's reach.

Enough time had passed for me to remember what Naomi had done. I stood abruptly, scrambled to grab the gun, and then shakily pointed it at her before she could take a step closer.

Out of my peripheral, I saw a large stone hurtling my way. After easily sidestepping out of its trajectory, I decisively waved the gun in her direction once again.

Naomi lifted her hands in surrender, her eyes trained on the barrel.

"How could you?!" I screamed at her.

She slightly lowered her hands to hold them out toward me, like trying to tame a wild animal.

"Raya, listen to me. Please. Yes, I was the one who got you on that stage, but I had to—"

We both ducked as shots rang out from a nearby guard, still holding his ground and shooting into the crowd.

"I only did what I did to help you. You have to believe that. I would never hurt you on purpose. You're my friend. You understand, right? Listen to me...Miss found out about Marie wanting to steal more weapons and Von faking a runaway attempt after torturing one of her servants. She knew all about the plan the entire time. She was going to quietly get rid of Marie and Von today without calling an assembly. I had to do something. You understand, right? You believe me?"

Naomi sounded crazed and desperate for my approved interpretation of her actions.

Without waiting for a response, she continued, "I warned Marie right before Miss came for you. She was still able to get everyone ready. The plan had to be adjusted, that's all. Please don't hate me."

Naomi was on the verge of tears and a mental breakdown, and I saw sincerity in her eyes.

I lowered the gun and stared at her in revelation.

All of the anger bubbling in my head began to fizzle out.

"I don't hate you," I simply replied, reasoning that I was still alive, which counted for something.

She smiled tearfully, reached for my hand, and pulled me toward the back of the yard while remaining low. We struggled to get through the thick mob of riled-up inmates, with the sound of their angry war cries ringing in my ears as they attacked the still-alive guards.

I looked up momentarily and saw Bertha, true to her word, swinging a food tray at Karen's head. The gruff woman called out for backup to no avail. She soon disappeared under the attacks of the women, and I could no longer hear her calling out for help.

"RAYA!"

Marie's voice suddenly cut through all of the violence as she called out to me with sheer determination.

In the hectic commotion, Naomi let go of my hand, but I continued to chase her through the crowd as I followed the sound of Marie's voice with my eyes.

"RAYA!" she bellowed again.

I searched frantically for her, but my feet slowed to a complete stop as my eyes landed on someone arrayed in head-to-toe black. It was someone formidable and...familiar.

He was carrying a disabled soldier tucked under his arm as if their weight was of little consequence. He was headed toward L block, where Farmer John was waiting and giving orders.

I blinked rapidly in disbelief.

Big Man?

Thirty-Seven

—·—

B IG MAN DISAPPEARED INTO the building with his chattel, mingling amongst others who were carrying injured soldiers of their own.

With Naomi gone...lost in the crowd, my feet were now forcing me in the direction of the building to confront the apparition.

Through the mayhem, I glimpsed another person in black, a girl I didn't recognize, firing at soldiers.

My eyes reverted again toward the building as another armed figure stumbled out. Her back was turned, but I'd recognize those big puffy curls anywhere.

Adina...

A whimper of happiness escaped my lips at the sight of her, and I began pushing harder to get out of the chaotic riot.

One more individual hobbled out behind her with his gun raised, ready to fire.

For a moment, I forgot how to breathe.

I started to tremble all over as I involuntarily pushed people aside to get to him. Scanning the area, he did a double take when he caught my eye and started recklessly shuffling in my direction despite the active gunfire.

My eyes must have been playing tricks on me, but before I could make sense of the mirage, he crashed into me, picking me up in a bear hug. My feet lifted from the ground, and he swung me around in a small circle.

Adina came rushing towards us but didn't stop until she was behind me. She pointed her gun toward the crowd, aiming at all the possible threats to protect our reunion.

Juda tried to put me down, but I couldn't handle my own weight. I interlocked my arms around his shirt collar, buried my face in his shoulder, and wept, "I saw you die...I saw you die. How—"

In a shaky voice, he whispered his answer near my ear, "Nothing is impossible with God..."

The heavy tears fell like a deluge of rain into the fabric of his sleek, black coat.

Praise You, Father...thank You, thank You, thank You!

Juda rocked me side to side as I blubbered incoherently.

"It's okay, Raya. Everything is gonna be okay."

"You came for me," I stammered out, still melting into his clothes.

"Of course I did. We would've been here sooner, but I had some things going on," he said jokingly.

The tears erupted again, but I could finally pilot my own legs, so I let go of the scruff of Juda's neck and stood before him with my hands clutched to my face, grinning like an idiot behind them.

"Juda!" Adina called over her shoulder. "Take it inside! I'll cover you. Nice to have you back, by the way, Raya."

Juda glanced warily at Adina before heeding her order. He took me by the hand and limped to the safety of the building.

Big Man emerged from deeper down the hall, empty-handed this time.

"Raya?" he voiced.

Never had I been so happy to hear Big Man speak...to hear any of *my people* speak. He came and draped his big arms around Juda and me.

"I can't believe you guys came for me," I sobbed again.

Big Man drew back.

"What? Of course, we came for you, girl," he drawled in his southern accent. "We came for everybody."

Big Man glanced defensively behind me and suddenly lifted his gun.

I turned around to see what was setting him on edge.

Adina was also holding her rifle up, but at Marie, who looked very pressed.

"I'm on your side! Raya...tell them," she pleaded as she caught my eye and shifted nervously.

"Wait. Guys, it's okay. That's Marie. Ryan's mom," I announced.

They lowered their weapons at my assurance.

"You okay, kid?" Marie asked, deflecting from the mention of Ryan as if it was too painful for her.

I nodded very fast, still in shock that I was alive.

"You?" I asked in return.

She nodded and regained her composure, but before she could say anything further, a man in a gray uniform came bustling through the door with an unconscious soldier in his arms.

The man didn't question or give a second glance to our gathering. He continued to the back until we could no longer see him.

"What are you guys doing with those soldiers?" I asked.

"We are locking up the survivors," Big Man answered. "It's not our right to decide their fate, but we need them out of the way for now."

"That's good," Marie mumbled more to herself before she spoke up again. "Make sure you take all their devices.

We don't want the other TRPs finding out what happened here. It'll make it harder for the others to escape."

Big Man nodded, though I could see confusion lining his face.

Marie turned towards the hallways and instructed us to come with her. I glanced up at Juda before shaking my head hesitantly. All I wanted to do was hide here with my brother.

"There are still people in the Chute. Rio could be there," she explained.

I straightened at that. The thought of poor, little Rio in the Chute made my stomach curdle and boil with disdain for anyone who would lock a four-year-old in that awful place.

"I'm going with Marie," I announced to the others.

"Then, I'm going, too," Juda stated, not letting go of my hand.

Adina instinctively moved toward us.

Big Man chose to stay, needing to destroy the soldiers' communication devices.

Marie took off with us in tow through the dark corridors leading to the Chute's elevator. She wielded a small lighter that barely illuminated the way.

When we reached it, she frantically pressed the button over and over to take us up, but nothing happened.

The door remained tightly shut, and we couldn't hear any mechanisms pulling the shaft up or down.

"All the power is disabled. We activated a temporary short-wave EMP," Juda explained to Marie.

Marie pointed to a nearby door, and when we went through it, even with the bare visibility, we could see stairs and plenty of them.

Juda looked at the steps apprehensively.

I could plainly see that my brother would have difficulty with them. Before I could suggest that Juda and Adina wait at the landing, we heard someone running towards us from a dim side corridor. Adina stepped protectively by Juda and raised her rifle towards the incoming sound.

Naomi shot through the intersecting hallways and tripped over herself when she saw us standing there. After regaining her footing, she stared wide-eyed at Juda, ignoring Adina completely.

"Hey, Naomi. I'm glad—"

She slapped the words right out of his mouth, then crashed into him, embracing him in a contradictory hug.

It happened so quickly that Juda had no time to react appropriately. He just stood there with his arms limp at his sides while she squeezed him. When she let go, it was as if he no longer existed again.

"Where are you going?" she asked me confrontationally.

I paused at her tone but decided that her unstable mental state warranted grace.

"Upstairs to the Chute. Rio might be there," I briskly answered.

She nodded and invited herself along.

"I'll stay here with Juda. If you aren't back in ten minutes—" Adina implied as if she would come to our rescue.

Marie gestured to wait inside the door in case anyone else unwarranted came barreling through the hallways.

Marie, Naomi, and I began our ascent, and when we reached the top after several minutes of running up and skipping steps, we were all overtired and out of breath. After gaining a second wind, Marie told us to check the Chute booths and ensure we freed everyone.

"I'll be right back," she managed.

The high windows encompassing the room provided just enough visibility, so Marie put away her tiny lighter. Even with the slight light filtering in through the windows, the Chute was darker than I remembered, its previous shadows consuming me with the horrible chantings.

Once trapped in this place, I wanted nothing more than the quiet enveloping us now. However, recalling when the silence finally came, it served only as a grim reminder of the torment. My thoughts took a life of their own, cruel echoes of demonic memories that didn't belong to me. Looking toward the booths, I was having severe Deja Vu.

"Rio?!" I shouted into the space.

Initially, there was only stillness mixed with foul odors of rot floating through the air, but as we approached, we began to hear people faintly calling out for help.

Naomi was stuck in place, shaken by the presence of the simplistic torture chambers, refusing to go near them.

Everything in me screamed to stay away, too, but I knew if we didn't get the people out, no one would likely return for them any time soon.

I mowed past my reservation and approached the box on the far left.

I fiddled with the lock, and when it finally popped open, the door swung out, allowing Von to exit. After he climbed out, he gave me an overwhelmingly energetic hug, then ran to the next box, letting another person out.

The sunken eyes of the prisoner widened at the sight of me and it took me a moment to recognize the terrorized face because of how much it had changed.

"Brother Isaiah?"

It was Drea's husband, and he looked physically ill and a thousand years older than he actually was.

"Thank you," he sniffled once he made it safely onto solid ground.

After seeing Von and Isaiah freed, Naomi finally shook off her reservations and went to the far right of the room to release the rest of the people trapped inside.

In total, three females and another male occupied the final booths, but Rio wasn't among them. They all had the same look of fear as they came out, but it quickly turned to perplexed joyfulness when they realized the fullness of the situation.

We all lingered there for a moment, a shared sense of achievement washing over us. The former prisoners reveled in the precious taste of freedom, not only for themselves or for the moment but for everybody outside and the future that lay ahead of them.

Suddenly a burst of laughter erupted from one of the women nearest Naomi. It began as a breathy chuckle but quickly escalated into an ecstatic cry, triumphant in every note. The sound reverberated through the eerie room, infecting each of us with a surge of emotion. Soon we were all laughing, unsure of exactly why, but then another thought took hold of me.

Rio!

"Naomi, where is Miss Agatha's room?" I asked abruptly, with no more laughter to spare.

She picked up on my reasoning and volunteered to go. She quickly left the foreboding Chute and headed for the stairs in search of Rio.

After she took off, I noticed Marie standing excitedly in front of one of the rooms in the corner furthest from the elevator. I hadn't noticed them weeks before when Miss pushed me towards my Chute experience.

The rooms were concealed, hidden in plain sight. Their gray doors blended into the gray wall. Marie was peering into a tiny window recessed into the door that had a keycard scanner next to it.

Marie, disregarding Juda's warning about the power, frantically swiped her keycard at the pad, with nothing happening. No lights or sounds were emitting from her efforts. She was starting to get frustrated and let out a barely audible scream.

She suddenly started searching her pockets and eventually pulled out a set of keys from the side of her camo uniform. After grappling to find the right one, she put the key in, and the door clicked open with little resistance.

Marie disappeared inside the room while we all looked on in anticipation. After an uncomfortably long wait, Marie emerged again but with a man lumbering at her side.

His gray long-sleeved uniform hung from his scrawny limbs like clothes on a wire hanger. His beard was mangled and matted, and his face showed the age of a wizen man, much like Brother Isaiah.

I was paralyzed to the spot as he emerged, and my legs threatened to give way. My pulse began to quicken beneath my skin, and time seemed to slow to a crawl. My heart lurched to a halt, frozen in a moment of disbelief.

It couldn't be.

Von noticed me wavering, so he grabbed the sides of my shoulders, centering me.

As I locked eyes with the man in shared astonishment, he whimpered softly, "Baby girl?"

His voice was brittle and cracked, but the tone was enduring.

"Dad?" my lips trembled out, choking on the word.

Marie confusedly looked between us.

"This is your dad?" she asked, but neither of us paid her any attention.

I instantly regained my strength and broke free from Von's grasp. Striding out to close the gap, I landed forcefully in my father's arms, causing him to shuffle backward slightly with a huff. He didn't seem to care about his frail physical state and embraced me with all the tenacity of an overcome parent, laughing and crying from joy.

Praise the Most High in heaven above!

Dad eventually released me from his grip but placed his arm around my shoulder, not only because he wanted to remain close but because he needed support. His once muscular physique had whittled down to chicken bones.

Marie secured his other arm around her neck, and we slowly made our way down the limitless amount of stairs.

The others went ahead as Von led them away. He was eager to reunite with his siblings. He still didn't know about Rio's absence, and I had no desire to tell him until after my own search concluded. Hopefully, Naomi would find her, and everything would be alright.

When we neared the bottom of the stairs, Marie struck her lighter back up, and we ambled towards the landing where Juda and Adina waited patiently. My dad's eyesight clearly had not failed him like his emaciated body.

"Juda? My boy—"

Juda glanced up to see who had addressed him.

When he caught sight of our father, his eyes glazed over with tears that threatened to escape, and he was trying hard not to let them.

Our father attempted to speak again, but his voice eluded him, imprisoned by the weight of his captivity. Instead, he struggled as he tried to extend his arm out toward his son without Marie's help.

Juda reached out and clung to him like a much-needed lifeline and praised God like I did when I first saw *him* only moments ago.

With my hands shielding my face, I laugh-cried at the sight of them, feeling like my heart would burst from overwhelming happiness.

Dad cringed suddenly and pulled away from Juda, who wasn't ready for the disconnect.

"Dad?"

His tired yet teary-eyed grin confirmed all was well, but he needed to rest.

"Let's get back out into the light," Marie interjected.

She didn't lead us back to L block but took a turn nearest the Chute elevator, and we were outside close to the front gate. The engraved letter above the block exit door read 'B.'

As soon as we made it out to the yard, we heard and saw inmates cheering in circular groupings.

Even though it was midday, the temperature had dipped considerably, and instead of everyone going back inside to get warm, they refused to step foot back into the hateful place.

Several people had already raided the Intake Center and the guard's barracks, and they were breaking apart wooden furniture and dousing papers with found gasoline to make bonfires.

Marie guided us to a blazing fire, and Juda carefully sat our father down in front of it. He stretched his arms out towards the glowing warmth of the blaze.

Wiping away tears, I looked through the crowd where reunions were happening all over the yard. Screams of joy and realization freely filled the air.

Coming from the Intake Center, Dark Shades...Tiffany...was holding little Rio's hand as Mateo and Von ran over to her, scooping her up and showering her in kisses.

Tiffany had removed her signature shades and did her best to remain indifferent, but she had weepy eyes from witnessing their reunion.

The scene all around me was prolific and felt like a dream. After all the suffering my people had endured, the glory truly belonged to the Most High.

He had delivered us.

THIRTY-EIGHT

— ❋ —

I HADN'T FELT TRULY safe for such a long time, but being wedged between my father and brother made me invincible.

Alive...they are both alive.

I sighed and curled up under my father's arm, watching as Juda continued throwing tiny sticks and leaves into the growing fire before us.

Every family sat around their makeshift bonfires, eagerly catching up for hours.

The sun was beginning to set, and the air was freezing, but that didn't bother a soul.

Everyone was too happy, too free, to notice the biting cold.

I looked up at my dad, who seemed to be the only one affected by the weather. He was shivering and holding onto his thin sleeves, his eyes ambiguously trained on Juda.

My brother met his gaze, smiling sincerely.

The warm fire lit up his face, making his grin more prominent as the other families sang praises loudly around us.

Finally, Juda gave up trying to feed the little fire and moved to sit on Dad's other side. He shook off his coat after noticing our father trembling uncontrollably and wrapped it around him.

Dad snapped out of whatever trance he'd been in before and began shaking his head violently.

"No," he said. "No, I can't take this from you, son. Just keep it. I'll be fine."

Juda seemed struck by his words but still managed to maintain the peaceful look plastered on his face.

"It's okay, Dad. I've got another one on the bus."

He blew out a frosty breath and patted him gently on the back.

Dad sighed in submission and seemed to retreat inside himself. I shifted from underneath his arm to take a better likeness of him.

"Daddy, are you okay?" I asked, mentally tracing the worry lines across his face.

It was a dumb question. I knew that.

My father had every right to feel numb after all he'd been through, but something about his current demeanor spoke to him being more than a bit off.

He nodded after a few seconds, but his eyes didn't agree with his gesture. He must have picked up on my apprehension because he further elaborated, "I guess I'm just...a little hungry."

Juda glanced at me briefly before giving his attention back to Dad.

"I've got some snacks back on the bus. I can bring them to you," he commented before his eyes shifted back to me. "You wanna come with me, Raya... to get the snacks?"

I shook my head, perfectly content to stay next to my father. An irrational fear gave birth inside me that if I let him out of my sight, he might disappear again.

Juda seemed beyond annoyed with my silent rejection to his request.

"Well, I really could use your help..." He tried again, this time his voice tight and low.

Oh.

Comprehending him, I stood up but bent down to kiss my father on the forehead before Juda dragged me away toward his bus.

He waited until we were out of earshot to start talking.

"Notice anything different about Dad?"

"Honestly...yeah. But doesn't it make sense? I don't think any of us are gonna be the same after this," I asserted.

Juda led me to the menacingly open gate, and I paused as we approached it. I watched as he easily walked beyond it like it was no big deal, but I couldn't move.

Juda stopped mid-stride when he no longer heard me walking behind him. He stepped back, holding onto the gate so he could lean inward.

"You coming?" he questioned, unsure why I paused in the first place.

I gulped and nodded, coming back to myself.

It's just a stupid gate.

I stepped through it hesitantly before following Juda a little ways down the road to where the bus was parked. The front end of it sustained heavy damage like they had used it for a battering ram against the gate.

"Here," Juda said once I caught up with him.

He held out his hand toward me, revealing a small yellow box.

"Solo told me to give this to you."

I opened it and smiled inwardly before taking the tiny mole device out, but Juda stopped me before I could attach it near my ear.

"Wait—" he started, but before he could give me a reason, the bus shook from the inside.

I froze in panic, fear dredging up from my insides.

I knew we shouldn't have left the gate...I knew it!

I braced myself for a fight but instantly let down my guard when I saw who emerged behind the bus door.

"Ryan?" I questioned meekly.

He looked different, but in a pleasing sort of way.

"Raya!" he warmly greeted, hopping from the last step off the bus.

Something inside me cringed, and I hovered closer to Juda like a shy child who needed protection. I might have been glad to see him under any other circumstance, but his presence now disturbed me.

"I'm so relieved that you're okay," Ryan called out, glancing behind him as a teenage girl and a little boy stepped off the bus, following him out.

The girl had milk chocolate skin, deep brown eyes, a naturally upturned nose, and six shoulder-length plaits hanging past her ears. The boy had her eyes, only they were more prominent, and his skin was like Solo's—tawny and bright.

Outside of Rio, he was the most adorable little person I'd ever seen.

He stood, peeking behind Ryan while pushing his floppy, loose curls away from his face.

Ryan explained stiffly, "Uh, Raya, these are my siblings. Dakota and Logan."

I forced a cautious smile and waved as politely as I could manage. I didn't have a problem with them.

My issue was with Ryan.

"It's nice to meet you finally," I maintained, "Ryan used to talk about you a lot."

The girl, Dakota, seemed to be faking her smile as well, but her facade seemed more from exhaustion and lack of energy for niceties.

"Only good things, I hope?" she said in a buttery child-like manner.

I cut my eyes at Ryan and then focused back on her. "Of course."

Juda, who had been scratching the back of his head awkwardly, decided to retreat onto the bus to get the snacks, leaving me with the strangers momentarily.

"—I wanted to keep them away from the fight," Ryan explained unsolicited while we waited for Juda to return.

I had no reply to offer.

A few painfully silent seconds went by before Ryan decided to speak again.

"Is my mom..." his words faded hopelessly before he could finish the sentence.

I nodded back toward the fence, "She's in there. Alive and well."

His face seemed to light up after that, and he began to walk away toward the gate with Dakota and Logan in tow before I stopped him.

His brother and sister continued, unaware that he wasn't with them.

Surprised, Ryan looked down at where my hand was gripping his coat sleeve.

"You lied to me," I accused in a low, constricted tone.

He stubbornly stared into my eyes before attempting to feign innocence.

"I don't know what you're talking about," he shrugged.

"Yes, you do. Don't—"

"Look, Raya. Not now, okay?"

"Then when? I trusted you," I seethed.

Ryan tore away from my grip, turning his face towards his brother and sister.

"I don't have to explain myself to you," he said before storming off.

I watched him enter the compound after his siblings, and they disappeared to the right.

I turned on my heels and stepped onto the bus when Juda emerged.

"You were right," I rashly huffed.

Juda blinked daftly.

"About what?" he asked, shrugging on his new coat.

"You..." I tried to find the words, raking my fingers through my cropped hair in frustration. "You were right about Ryan. About everything, and I—"

Juda cut me off by pulling me into an unexpected hug. In an instant, the built-up anger and hysteria faded away.

"Just calm down, Raya," Juda purred smoothly before he let me go. "Now, what's this about?"

I took in an icy breath and released it before starting over.

"Ryan," I explained slowly. "He's a liar. He lied. You were right about him. I never should have trusted him. What are we gonna do?"

Juda listened with his hands on his hips before he swiped at his brow and laughed.

"What? What's funny right now?"

He shook his head, still smiling.

"Give the guy a break, Raya. Nobody's perfect."

Juda shouldered his bag of snacks and moved past me, and I followed close behind him in complete and utter disbelief.

"Juda, I'm telling you that you were right. Ryan lied about stuff, and now he's being defensive about it. He really could be dangerous, and now you're laughing at me," I argued to his back.

Juda turned to face me after getting a few steps away from the bus.

"Raya," he baited, "Ryan jumped in front of a bullet to save *you*. Remember that? If he wanted to hurt anybody, I'm sure he would have done it by now. Please just leave it alone."

I puffed out a sarcastic laugh, crossing my arms.

"I don't understand. You literally seemed ready to fight me over this whole 'Ryan' situation a few months ago, but now that I'm actually agreeing with you, I'm the bad guy? Why are you acting so...different?"

Juda sighed, "I'm not."

"You are."

"No, I'm acting better, not different."

"Juda, what does that even mean right now?"

He seemed to be struggling with his answer as he stared past me.

"Juda—"

"When I was in a coma for a month, Raya...while I was out, I saw..." He started but trailed off into silence.

"What? What did you see?"

He sighed heavily, blowing out iced smoke.

"Nevermind. That's not important. The point is that all this is bigger than me. It's bigger than you...and it's way bigger than Ryan. I think I'm ready to just be okay with that."

Juda continued walking again when I couldn't think of an adequate reply. The only sound between us was crunching against the frozen dirt with our shoes.

When I finally thought to speak, Juda beat me to it.

"It's not just that though," he ranted, "I mean, I was actually wrong about many things. And I was selfish. I didn't want to accept it before, but now I understand, and I want to support you and your mission because that's bigger than me, too. You just let me know where I can help."

My eyes began to water, and I anxiously wrung my cold, dry hands in front of me.

"There is no mission. You weren't wrong about that. I thought I could do it. I thought I was strong, but I'm not. I know that now. I'm just a kid."

"Raya—"

"No. I just...I just want it to be over, okay? We got Dad. That's more than we could've ever hoped for. I just want things to go back to normal. I just want to go home."

When we returned to the gate's threshold, the feeling of unease attacked me again.

Before, I had been afraid to walk out. Now, I was scared to go back in.

Juda placed his hands on my shoulders and turned me to face him. He lowered himself to eye level with me.

"Raya, listen, you are the bravest, strongest, most selfless...and annoying person I know, okay? You think because you had to endure a storm, it changes who you are or what you've accomplished, but it doesn't. You survived it, so that makes you stronger. And look around you. Look at all those people out there with their families. How do you not see the Most High using you? You have a gift, Raya. You move and inspire people. We got work to do, aight? You started something. Now you need to finish it."

I wiped the tears from my face with my dingy coat sleeve and didn't offer any reply.

Juda started walking again, and I reluctantly followed him through the gate.

I looked around and watched all the families enjoying each other's company.

I saw Shiri with her parents.

Her mother stroked her hair gently as her father locked her in his embrace for the eightieth time.

I saw Drea and Isaiah hanging onto each other, refusing to be separated again.

Big Man had found his sister, Anedra, and she laughed while he reenacted their quest to Mississippi.

I saw Juda pat Dad on the back as he plopped down next to him in front of the small fire.

And I saw Mateo.

He lovingly played rock, paper, scissors with Rio, tussling her hair in approval whenever she beat him. Von was peeling her an orange that he'd swiped from one of the guard's barracks. Mateo's radiant smile at his little sister was infectious, causing me to beam a broad smile their way.

As if he could sense someone watching them, he glanced up, caught my eye, and waved.

I was beginning to lift my hand and wave back when suddenly, a loud, manic shriek broke out through the air.

I turned toward the noise, my heart jumping in my throat.

What now...

The sound had come from a woman standing by another more significant fire not too far from where my family rested. She was holding a big ball of prison uniforms above her head, and a crowd formed around her.

I jogged toward the commotion.

"—And burn the clothes of our oppression!"

I caught the tail end of Leah's speech.

Marie moved towards the scene with her kids and Tiffany following close behind.

Leah threw the clothes into the fire before Marie could stop her. The crowd of people cheered around her, and the fire grew.

The corners of my mouth almost tilted up at the sight.

All those months of washing the foul-smelling gray uniforms...I had half a mind to rip mine off and throw it in as well.

It seemed like a lot of other people had that same thought by the looks on their faces.

Marie, however, did not.

She practically screamed as she pushed through the crowd to get to Leah.

"Hey!" she yelled. "Listen! Everybody! You can't burn your clothes! There's too many of us to bus out tonight, and we still have to figure out where we're all going, so we might be here for a while!"

The entire establishment got quiet momentarily, and then suddenly, it wasn't.

Everybody broke out in angry questioning.

I looked through the crowd at Juda, who was standing now. He looked back at me before he helped Dad up.

Marie grabbed my arm and pulled me away from what had turned into a mob.

"You need to do something," she demanded.

Me? What can I do?

Understanding suddenly draped across my body, and in that spirit, I jumped onto Miss' raised platform to address the people.

"Listen! Please, listen!" I bellowed with my hands to the crowd in a 'calm down' motion.

Everyone quieted to hear me speak.

Only a few hushed whispers resonated through the crowd.

"There are other TRPs out there, and the Syndicate will not stop hunting our people down just because this one fell! We are free today, sure, but until the entire Program is stopped, we will never truly be free! This is bigger than us leaving here today. We are one body, one force, and with the Most High for us, who can stand against us?! Please be patient. We need to plan. Time is irrelevant. Can't you see that? We move in God's timing...not our own! That's the only way we succeed. Please, listen to her—" I yelled while pointing to Marie.

She took over and started to explain that there were safe places across the States that we could all disperse to, but it would take time and proper planning.

As her voice faded into my background, I returned to where Juda and my father stood.

"Raya...where is your mole comm? Put it on. Solo wants to talk to you," Juda announced as I approached.

I had forgotten all about the contents of the tiny yellow box still clutched in my hand. Taking out the black speck of a radio again, I placed it near my ear.

"Hello?"

Solo invaded my thoughts in that unnerving way I disliked, "Hey, cousin. I missed you."

I couldn't handle any more tears, but at the sound of his voice, my eyes breamed with them anyway, and my lips quivered.

We talked for a few blissful minutes before Solo hesitated.

"What's wrong, Solo?" I ordered, intuitively sensing something had happened.

"Um...the Syndicate is playing a recorded message on a national broadcast. Hold on..."

"They must have figured out the TRP has fallen by now," I reasoned.

"No, it isn't that—"

He paused for an incredibly long time.

"What is it then?" I all but barked.

"The message...it's from your mom."

Epilogue

— ❖ —

Naomi

I WATCHED MISS SPEAK enthusiastically while I stood far away at the M-block entryway.

Raya kneeled next to her with her head bowed low, graciously accepting her fate.

I felt a tinge of guilt for placing her there, but I was content knowing that no matter what happened today, I would be free.

As Agatha yelled out to the assembly about hope, I recalled my first encounter with her when she said something similar.

It happened a week after being caught in the woods on account of Drea.

I was learning my way around the big industrial kitchen, and admittedly, I was still enraged at her and the rest of the world.

As a newbie, it was my job to dispose of the abominable meats the cooks refused to use. I was instructed to hide the clear bag of discarded meat inside a service cart between stacks of trays and hand it off to a grumpy-looking female guard at the end of the hallway.

She must have been sympathetic to our plight but never showed it in her demeanor.

That was my daily assignment.

At the end of that first week, I walked the rotten bag of meat towards the handoff point, but before I could make it, two soldiers approached and demanded that I come with them.

When I tried to balk and make excuses about not leaving the service cart, they made me bring it along.

My destination, reluctantly, had been detoured to Miss Agatha's personal quarters.

She was having lunch with a man who looked faintly familiar, but I couldn't quite place him. He was sitting at the other end of her long table, quietly eating his meal.

Miss had situated her dining area to imitate a fancy ballroom with inmates stationed every few feet. It seemed she employed them as personal servants because they stood at attention, steadfast and stoic, anticipating her every need.

When I was forced into the room with my cart, she did not immediately acknowledge my presence. Instead, she continued to address the mysterious man in the all-black suit.

"—Please call me Miss. Doctor sounds so...clinical."

The man coughed faintly and responded in a monotone voice, "If that's what you prefer. But Dr. Rainer...I mean...Miss. How does this work? The Department of Homeland Security has shelled out millions of dollars for the operation of your facilities. Still, I haven't been able to present any solid evidence that the Program is or ever will work. I will have to have some proof by the end of the year."

Miss looked up from her plate of ribeye steak, fresh steamed broccoli, and baked potato, then laid down her knife and fork with a soft clang of the metal on porcelain.

"Then let me explain the premise of my Program to you, Phillips. It's quite simple, really. You will have your proof soon enough."

She cleared her throat and began, "To socially influence an entire culture for generations to come...mass deconstruction of their perceived reality must occur."

She paused to wipe her mouth with the cloth napkin one of the servants stepped up and provided.

"The first course of action in this process is always involuntary submission. Thus, the TRP facilities are necessary. Detrimental, even."

She threw the napkin across her unfinished food.

"The second step is to introduce a distorted alternate chain of thought that blocks the spiritual link from the creation to the assumed creator. One must lack purpose. That's where the Chute excels."

Miss stood up and leaned against the table to explain her last point.

"The final...and key...detail to solidifying this new standard is manipulating and manufacturing a new idol to emulate. Monkey see, monkey do. Do you understand?"

As she crossed the room to where I stood, still at a loss as to what was happening, Phillips did not debate her and watched intently as she approached me.

"Speaking of new idol..."

Miss cupped my chin tightly in her right hand while examining my perplexed face.

"I saw the way she looked at you in line. She cares for you. You two must be close friends. That's good. That's useful to me...so I suppose you'll do," Miss calculated out loud.

My hands still gripped the service cart while she stared into my eyes with ungodly determination.

Her manner turned sour suddenly, and she began sniffing the air, trying to source an offensive odor.

"What is that atrocious smell?" she asked as she searched the cart until she located the bag of pork intestines and fatback.

She picked up the bag and scrutinized it, then placed it back where she found it, covering it up again.

She turned and meandered past Phillips, who was watching the scene with earnest interest at this point.

After reaching a wooden side server, she demanded that I come.

My heart began to pound in anticipation as I let go of the cart, obeying her command.

Once I was within arm's reach, she picked up a truncheon conveniently placed on top of the server, extended it with a flick of her wrist, and began striking me with unnatural precision.

I recoiled, trying to protect myself, but she hit me in all directions until I fell to the floor, defensively curling up in a fetal ball.

She struck me until all I could hear was ringing in my ears. I lay there in incredible agony when she retracted the weapon, laying it gracefully back in its place.

Miss then walked back to her seat, and another servant pushed up her chair after she sat down again. She took the napkin away from her plate, draped it across her lap, and finished her meal casually.

Phillips gave a wistful smirk at her display of ruthless lunacy.

As her fork scraped across the plate again, she addressed him, "Oh yes, where was I? Ah...I forgot to mention one caveat to this entire experiment."

"And what's that?" he quizzically replied, watching her eat peacefully.

"Hope, my dear Phillips."

"Hope? That's trivial, Dr. Rainer," he sneered at her senseless conclusion.

"On the contrary...the only way to reverse my reculturing program is to give the subjects hope. With it, they will fight against the three pillars of reconstruction. They will buck the system and rise against their forced mental collapse. In its absence, however, there is acceptance and conformity to new, extreme norms—"

As she spoke, I sputtered and coughed loudly to regain my breath and sight. Small black and white stars danced across my vision. The pain was fascinatingly acute.

Without looking back at me, Miss finished expounding her hypothesis to her guest, "With hope, they will seek salvation."

She then requested that the soldiers standing at the door remove me to the Chute and roll my cart back to the kitchen.

She announced that they were to give every worker on shift a demerit for trying to discard the good enough meat that the Commander had so kindly provided. She told the soldiers to also make the staff aware that the demerit was compliments of me.

While being forcefully removed by the guards, I called out several times that this should be my first demerit, to which Miss simply replied, "But you, Naomi, are now on my...accelerated program."

Within days of the encounter, I was moved to her quarters, where I and three other people had to rotate sleeping on the floor at the foot of her bed.

She had fetters fashioned to the ground to chain us up, ensuring we didn't try anything threatening during the night.

Sometimes, she would have a fit in the early morning hours, which was a guaranteed beating out of our already fretful sleep.

I thought back to every time she would pretend to treat me as an equal, offering tidbits like oranges or candies, but as soon as I let go of my service cart, her behavior switched, and she would thrash me or declare the Chute as a punishment.

I was conditioned never to leave my post...the cart.

After the altercation between Raya and the guard, Miss started to gravitate towards Rio as a potential manipulative. She would go on and on about how she would show the world her genius through Raya, who was her target idol all along.

My fate was sealed after I choked Raya in the hallway.

I did it not only because her carelessness would cost me a day in the Chute for spilling Miss' favorite dessert, but I also did it out of resentment for being singled out as Raya's friend.

Miss decided that Rio would be my perfect replacement and eventually put her in solitary confinement in a hidden cage at the Intake Center.

She was so proud of herself for killing two birds with one stone. Use Rio to get Raya to cooperate and present Rio to Phillips as her evidence that the Program was a proven success.

That left me at a crossroads with Miss Agatha.

I knew too much for her to release me back into the general population, but I was useless to her as a means to an end.

The night before Liberation Day, Miss had a frightful fit in the middle of the night.

I thought she would succeed in pummeling me to death, so to save myself and prove that I was still valuable, I blurted out that Raya was planning a revolt the next day at noon. I gave up Von as her co-conspirator, and she immediately called the guards to lock him in the Chute.

"I was wrong about you, Naomi," she comforted and stroked my hair while I crouched cowardly next to her.

"Maybe you are the idol I was looking for all along."

Now, staring at Raya on the stage, I had two alternatives before me.

If she managed somehow to succeed with Liberation Day, I would throw myself at her mercy and help in any way possible. Or, if she died, Miss would transpose her desire for an idol onto me, and I would be free of this current mistreatment.

After Raya surprisingly did not die, I did exactly as planned and rushed to her side. She seemed to forgive me somewhat and even asked for my help to find Rio after we freed everyone in the Chute.

I did as she asked and went to Miss Agatha's quarters for the last time purposefully.

While I already knew Rio would not be found there, I went anyway to raid Agatha's stash of fruit that she always cruelly denied me.

Alone in her dining room, I picked out a rather ripe-looking green apple and popped a few grapes into my mouth. As I rummaged for the best-looking ones, I suddenly heard movement under the table.

I dropped my prize and looked to the server for the truncheon that I knew would be faithfully there.

After retrieving it, I walked cautiously around the table, peeking to see who had made it their hiding place.

To my bewilderment, Agatha, with her hair in a wild display of disorder, looked out to me, wide-eyed and relieved that it was I who found her.

"Oh, Naomi! Thank goodness...help me up. My leg..." she exclaimed while reaching out for assistance.

Straightening myself, I extended the truncheon and disclosed, "You know, Miss...I loved what you said about hope...it truly is a dangerous thing..."

Acknowledgements

All scriptures read or mentioned were quoted from the King James Version of the Holy Bible.

A special acknowledgment to the pastor of The Free Church of Christ, based in Sugar Hill, GA. All sermons or biblical conversations were derivative from prior devotional excerpts, with expressed permission.

All song and musical references were used with the expressed permission of the artist mentioned.

To our family and friends who endured through this journey with us, a million thanks. A special thank you to Kim Abrams and Gigi Abrams-Craven, whose influence touched these pages more than they will ever know.

And as always, the utmost gratitude to Margit Hutton for her incredible support in editing and being a consistent volunteer as the first beta reader for each novel. Without her keen eyes, we would be lost.

ABOUT THE AUTHORS

Cheyenne Nikole is a bestselling teen indie author of the Chosen Trilogy, a biblically-inspired dystopian fantasy series. She is a high school graduate from Liberty University Online Academy. Cheyenne loves all things Young Adult dystopian and had the vision for this story based on her personal faith mixed with her love of post-apocalyptic literature. She currently resides with her family in Atlanta, Georgia.

Elisabeth Fowler is a bestselling indie author of The Chosen Trilogy, a biblically-inspired dystopian fantasy series. She has a degree in Consumer Sciences, concentrating in Financial Planning, and has spent over 15 years in the corporate insurance profession. Leaving her corporate career behind, Elisabeth's mission is to challenge readers to find the hidden social messages tucked within the pages of speculative literature. When Elisabeth isn't crafting fictional allegories, she enjoys traveling the world.

Originally from Tuscaloosa, Alabama, and now living in Atlanta, Georgia, Elisabeth resides with her husband and three beautiful children.

Also By

Survival House by Elisabeth Fowler

The Chosen Trilogy: Sanctuary (Book 1)

Syndicate: Ryan's Beginnings
Coming Soon!

The Chosen Trilogy: S.O.S (Book 3)
Coming Soon!

Link to books and blog:
https://www.liswritesthewrongs.com

SYNDICATE: RYAN'S BEGINNINGS

— ❖ —

COMING SOON!

Dakota

I N THE PITCH BLACK of early morning, I groaned at the thought of getting up just to use the bathroom. It took me hours to get comfortable, and my anxious mind kept me from falling asleep easily, but now it was the urge to pee that continued to nag at me. I shifted irritably out of bed, envying Kristen, who slept peacefully in hers.

Even though she was situated across the room and had the superpower of falling asleep at will, I slipped out of the room quietly to avoid waking her. Tip-toeing down the hall to the bathroom, I grimaced at the unwelcoming brightness of the lights after flipping on the switch.

It didn't take me long to get in and out, though.

There was still this lingering hope that if I hurried, I could get back in bed and continue where I left off, skipping all the tossing, turning, and telling my thoughts to shut up for three more hours.

But I never made it back to bed.

I heard sniffling as I passed my brother's room, so I paused curiously in front of the door to listen a bit closer.

I could hear my baby brother whimpering softly and babbling about something I couldn't quite make out. My bed was calling me, and I would've kept going if he hadn't sounded so distressed.

He shared his room with our oldest sibling, Ryan, so it baffled me that it sounded as if no one was already there to comfort him.

I rapped lightly on the door and waited.

When I got no response, I pushed the door open to confirm my suspicion. Logan was curled underneath his Spider-Man covers, trembling and afraid.

He was also very much alone.

Where is Ryan?

"Please don't take me—" my brother cried out as I rushed to his side.

"Shh...Lolo, it's me," I whispered, crouching beside his bed.

Peeking out from the covers, his curly head emerged, and his big brown eyes widened when he realized it was only me. He immediately let down his guard and wrapped his arms around my neck, breaking into fresh tears.

I held his embrace and stroked his silky curls to console him.

"What's the matter?" I asked softly, drawing back to look at his face.

With his window strangely open, the moonlight seeped in and brightly illuminated his silhouette. Logan hated having the window open at night, especially in early spring when the air was full of dampness. I reasoned that the window was likely the cause of his unwarranted fears.

His tawny cheeks were tear-stained, and he kept hiccupping on his frequent sniffles.

"I—I'm scared. There's something..." he stammered.

"There's what? Where's Ryan?" I glanced over at his empty bed and sighed deeply.

It was flawlessly made and appeared completely untouched.

I knew something had been bothering him for a while, but it was starting to get out of hand. I was beginning to think it was time to tell Marie and Dad because Ryan wasn't the type to sneak out at night.

Now, poor Logan was caught in the middle of it.

"Ryan said...he would be back later, but—" Logan tried again with his words before sucking in another big shaky breath.

He seemed to calm immensely as he exhaled.

"That's good, Lolo. Just breathe."

He took another deep breath and sighed.

"I had a bad dream."

I sat beside him, crossed my legs, and gripped his hands.

"Do you wanna talk about it?" I invited.

He shook his head, making his chestnut-colored curls sway from side to side.

"Well, did you pray?"

Ashamed, Logan looked down at our interlocked hands. His tears started freefalling again, but he remained silent this time.

"Lolo?" I implored and gently nudged his chin up, making him face me.

I desperately wanted to reassure him that he had no reason to be afraid, but even I felt something was off.

"In my dream...there was somebody outside. I'm scared, and I miss Ryan," he whimpered, burying his head into my shirt.

Somebody outside?

I looked cautiously toward his open window. Maybe he just wanted the window closed, and his imagination got the best of him.

"It's okay, little bro. Look—" I peered into his doe-sized eyes. "You're going to be alright. I'm gonna close the window, and we'll pray, okay? Then, you need to go back to sleep. It's a school night."

He sniffed and nodded, haphazardly swiping snot and tears from his face.

I got up and shuffled toward the open window but paused in panic when I saw a black SUV parked in our driveway.

It was where Ryan's red Camaro should have been.

Four menacing-looking men dressed in all black with ski masks covering their faces climbed out of the vehicle.

"Kota?" Logan whispered, picking up on my hesitation.

My body was ignited with dread and confusion. Not knowing how to react, I stood there frozen, watching as three of the men marched toward our front door and out of my line of sight.

Adrenaline kicked in when the one still lingering by the SUV abruptly looked up at me. Instinct took over my reflexes when our eyes met, and he made the gun fingers sign at the window.

POW.

There was a blasting crash downstairs.

The gesture and the smashing sound of glass seemed to work together. How in sync it all was.

I quickly jumped away from the window just in time to cover Logan's scream with my hand.

They're in the house, and they know we're awake.

Like a mental index, all the movies and true crime documentaries I'd ever watched flashed through my mind's eye.

Robbers won't usually attack if you're asleep...right?

But we weren't asleep, at least, not Logan and me.

I grabbed my little brother and hauled him toward the closet with my hand still tightly covering his mouth.

My heart picked up speed as booted footsteps crept up the stairs. Maybe I wouldn't have heard them under any other circumstance, but it was like my whole body and all my senses were hyper-focused.

My only determination was to stay alive.

Logan had no issue with me stuffing him into his walk-in closet. We crawled to the very back end, frantically pushing the low-hanging clothes out of the way to reach Ryan's old trap door.

Once I could open the secret compartment, I pushed Logan inside and crawled in after him, pulling the clothes back in their original position before securing the tiny trap door.

The small space was painted a rich sky blue on the inside. Once upon a time, illuminated by purple LED lights hidden underneath the fake cotton clouds that Ryan had thought to tape to the walls. Worn-out glow-in-the-dark stars that were too old to work anymore were stuck to the low ceiling. Even though I couldn't see them, I knew they were there because no one dared to remove anything from our special hiding place.

Ryan wouldn't allow it.

He, Kristen, and I used to love playing here when we were small enough to all fit. It should have felt like a safe haven, but it was giving off a creepy, dank vibe now that we were hiding for our lives.

I cradled Logan in my arms and sat uncomfortably restricted in the small space. With my back against the innermost wall, my heart drummed loudly in my ears. I was irrationally afraid the sound of its thumping would give us away.

We heard another loud crash, but closer down the hallway this time. Logan jumped and made a slight noise.

I swiftly leaned by his ear and shushed him, holding him tighter.

We were both jolted in alarm at the pop of nearby gunshots and then the agonizing sound of Marie screaming at the top of her lungs.

"MOM!"

Was that Ryan's voice?

Tears began to stream down my face. My breathing seemed to speed up, and I squeezed Logan a little too tightly.

Feet were thundering through the house now. Things were crashing and breaking. Then I suddenly remembered that my sister was fast asleep in our room where I left her.

Kristen!

I let go of my brother in realization that Kristen was still out there exposed. Logan gasped for air immediately.

I needed to get to her.

I needed to help.

"Stay here and don't make a sound," I whispered faintly, crawling back toward the little door.

Logan desperately clawed at the hem of my shirt, pulling me back with a surprisingly strong grip.

"Don't leave me," he begged, his eyes wide in terror.

I could barely see, but from what I could tell, the look on his face was pleading and wild. I was torn between staying and going, but the decision was soon made for me when Logan's bedroom door slammed open full force into the adjoining wall.

I jerked backward, hitting my head against the cotton clouds, but the sound of boots seemed to cover the noise.

Logan gasped and almost cried out, but I covered his mouth again with my arm, pushing us up against the wall and whispering just above a breath for him to calm down and be extra still.

"It's okay. We're okay," I muttered softly.

"—Are you sure?" a gruff-sounding man spoke out in the middle of the room.

"Yeah, I saw her in the window. But it could have been that girl across the hall. Looked like her."

"Search the room anyway. The boss said no survivors."

With my free hand, I covered my own mouth and went back to squeezing the life out of Logan when the closet door burst open. We could hear the man clawing aggressively through the clothes, searching for me.

I took no chances.

I held my breath, shut my eyes, and dug my hand into Logan's lips.

One wrong move, and we're dead.

Made in the USA
Columbia, SC
06 May 2025

57577425R20245